Fellow Travelers

New World Studies
Marlene L. Daut, Editor

Fellow Travelers

How Road Stories Shaped the Idea of the Americas

John Ochoa

University of Virginia Press
Charlottesville and London

University of Virginia Press
© 2021 by the Rector and Visitors of the University of Virginia
All rights reserved
Printed in the United States of America on acid-free paper

First published 2021

9 8 7 6 5 4 3 2 1

Library of Congress Cataloging-in-Publication Data
Names: Ochoa, John A. (John Andres), author.
Title: Fellow travelers : how road stories shaped the idea of the Americas / John Ochoa.
Description: Charlottesville : University of Virginia Press, 2021. | Series: New World studies | Includes bibliographical references and index.
Identifiers: LCCN 2020058648 (print) | LCCN 2020058649 (ebook) | ISBN 9780813946078 (hardcover) | ISBN 9780813946085 (paperback) | ISBN 9780813946092 (ebook)
Subjects: LCSH: Fiction—20th century—History and criticism. | Travelers' writings—History and criticism. | Travel writing—History—20th century. | Travel in literature. | Male friendship in literature. | America—Literatures—History and criticism.
Classification: LCC PN846 .O28 2021 (print) | LCC PN846 (ebook) | DDC 809/.897—dc23
LC record available at https://lccn.loc.gov/2020058648
LC ebook record available at https://lccn.loc.gov/2020058649

This book is freely available in an open access edition thanks to TOME (Toward an Open Monograph Ecosystem)—a collaboration of the Association of American Universities, the Association of University Presses, and the Association of Research Libraries—and the generous support of the Pennsylvania State University. Learn more at the TOME website, available at: openmonographs.org.

This book is licensed under the Creative Commons Attribution 4.0 International License (CC BY), https://creativecommons.org/licenses/by/4.0/legalcode.

https://doi.org/10.52156/m.5239

Cover art: *Aurora* (*Entre dos luces*), Juan Manuel Blanes, ca. 1879–1885. (Photo © Christie's Images/Bridgeman Images)

For Jack and Pablo Eduardo,
Fellow travelers if there ever was a pair

Contents

To the Reader: An Outstretched Hand   ix

Acknowledgments   xi

Introduction: Together, through the Backcountry   1

1. Fools of Empire: A Morning Constitutional, or Blind Eyewitnesses in the Early Republics (H. H. Brackenridge's *Modern Chivalry* and Alonso Carrió de la Vandera's *A Guide for Blind Travelers*)   31

2. Dying Pastoral: The Power of Homology and Other Disappearances into the Open Range of *Martín Fierro* and *The Searchers* (and "Brokeback Mountain")   57

3. The Size of Domesticity 1: Traveling Companions Flee from Cold War "Containment" in *On the Road* and *The Motorcycle Diaries*   78

4. The Size of Domesticity 2: Subcomandante Marcos's On-the-Run Dispatches Repurpose Cold War Anxiety   96

5. Doesn't He Ever Learn? Denis Johnson's *Jesus' Son* and the Weight of Knowledge, or a Second Chance for a Lonely Picaro   120

Notes   133

Works Cited   143

Index   153

To the Reader: An Outstretched Hand

Do the Americas have a common history? Do they have a common literature? These are questions that seem to be asked at least every fifteen years but are only partially answered.[1] Although there is still very much work to be done, some recent scholars have made considerable advances in hemispheric American literature and in comparative intellectual, literary, and cultural histories. I can only claim to imitate the remarkable breadth of scholars such as Lois Parkinson-Zamora, Kirsten Silva Gruesz, Ralph Bauer, Jorge Cañizares Esguerra, Emily Fox, and Anna Brickhouse.

This book about fellow travelers is an invitation extended by a Latin Americanist to anyone willing to find, and survey, some common yet unexplored ground: to travel together. (North) Americanists and Latin Americanists have too much in common and too much to lose if we do not walk and talk with one another. My hope is to deepen—or, in some cases, simply to begin—a traveling conversation.

I recognize that I speak (US) American literary studies with an accent and inevitably fumble some of its conventions or blindly walk past some of its milestones. But I believe *Fellow Travelers*'s deliberate combination of a broad scope and a fairly narrow theme justifies some methodological and disciplinary liberties, as well as some "outsiderhood." I hope the license I've taken (and any blemishes) will be understood.

The point of *Fellow Travelers* is to find places and ways that are at once familiar and unfamiliar, as happens in travel—especially travel through the backcountry. In terms of history and cultural specificity, I have aimed for cases of not-always-obvious homology. Basically, the overarching and guiding principle has been to locate striking similarities—which in turn warrant analogy and, I hope, productive comparison. This was my criterion for the selection of texts, as well as the method of inquiry.

For instance, when I address the late colonial/early republican period, I follow the lead of works such as Jorge Cañizares-Esguerra's comparative history *Puritan Conquistadors,* written about an earlier historical period. I place side by side two apparently unrelated historical processes that had similar impact on North and South during the period I am considering: the Spanish Decrees of Free Trade of 1778 (which opened the Spanish colonies to international trade) and the process of republican formation in the early United States, whereby distinct ex-colonies and their various social classes were incorporated into one representational system. In different ways, these two processes were equally necessary for the invention of independent, sovereign America(s), and both were deeply connected to the process of independence.

Likewise, when I approach national expansion into the contested empty spaces during the later nineteenth century, I look at the US mythology about the conquest of the West. But I do so through the lens of Argentinean gaucho culture, which conquered the wilderness at roughly the same time. The *gauchesque,* the foundational literary genre of modern Argentina, has so much in common with US Western culture that it honestly mystifies me that this hasn't been commented upon more.

There are many, many such cases of unexplored North/South homologies, and I only draw upon a few in this book. In the course of my argument, I often point to some of the homologies that clearly fall outside of the purview of *Fellow Travelers* but deserve further study, and I welcome more work in that direction. In addition, in several of my comparative case studies I have required the existing criticism itself to travel, applying insights about the cultures of the North to texts and objects of the South, and vice versa.

As the Mexican scholar, poet, and essayist Alfonso Reyes once said, among the lot of us we know everything. With *Fellow Travelers* I hope to expand who is included in "the lot of us," and perhaps even discover something beyond the "everything"—something more to know, and talk about, together. *Adelante.*

Acknowledgments

LIKE READING obituaries and wedding announcements, compact and charged, reading book acknowledgments can produce anything from admiration to incredulity, from twinges of envy to snorts of "I-knew-it." Let's admit it: who can truly claim never to have tossed aside a promisingly titled book after a scan of the acknowledgments? Here is my contribution to this unsettling genre, where I hope to express my honest gratitude to some folks, but also show off a lineage about which I am proud.

I invite potential readers to use this as a pre-vetting for what comes ahead.

The editor in chief at the University of Virginia Press, Eric Brandt, was supportive and bafflingly loyal to this project from the outset. This was despite major holdups, any of which would have made a reasonable book wrangler give up, and quite understandably. Thanks as well to managing editor Ellen Satrom, whose humor and caring make my previous experiences pale in comparison. *Repetidas gracias,* Eric and Ellen.

The first stirrings of *Fellow Travelers* came many nights ago in graduate school, inspired by two very different people and scholars, Roberto González Echevarría and Josefina Ludmer. It took twenty years to see the common ground in what they were then working on, respectively, the picaresque and the gauchesque. As often happens when one ventures out into unknown parts, this led down some arduous paths that led nowhere. I first believed this would be a long book about constitutionality, so following that belief, I consulted heavily with law scholars, especially David Flatto, Michael C. Mirow, and Lauren Benton, who shared their expertise and insight, but ultimately made me understand that this needed to go elsewhere.

For this being a book about men, it was guided most crucially by the advice and encouragement of four women, each fiercely intelligent and right. Lois Parkinson Zamora, a true inter-Americanist, has been a constant and rare guide for how to do and be both as a person and an intellectual. Giuli Dussias, friend and head of the department of Spanish, Italian, and Portuguese at Penn State, besides personally holding herself to a standard that is nigh impossible to repeat, provided an overwhelming amount of assistance and leeway. My wife, Stacy Andersen, MD and PhD (in literature, no less), has always been an exacting perceiver of hidden patterns—a master diagnostician. My friend and PSU colleague Maria Rosa Truglio has been a constant fellow traveler, willing to walk wherever. Each of these women has received a hand-loomed Mexican *rebozo* as expression of my thanks, and with the hope that they will continue telling me what (not) to do.

An unflagging and constant research assistant, Emily Wiggins, has for years conscientiously wrangled unruly language, data, sources, and images, among many unreasonable requests. She almost deserves a coauthorship. Copyeditor Phyllis Elving fine-combed pretty much all the prose. An undergraduate student, Panini Pandya, helped out at the very end. Eric Hayot and Tom Beebee at Penn State read and commented on the overarching plan during key junctures of development, putting quite some effort into helping me hammer it all out.

I have always depended on running conversations with Ernesto Livón Grosman and Nina Gerassi, spread out over the years and with regrettably long pauses. Among many other things, Ernesto helped me approach Argentina, his once-and-future home. *Nos debemos un viaje juntos.* Aníbal González, Priscila Meléndez, Catalina Villar Ruiz, Linda Kleindorfer, and Jennifer Siegel have always looked out for me, and I'm glad to have found Dina Rivera again.

Light conversations or casual email exchanges, often apparently random or unrelated, resonated and held: with Catharine Wall, Vera Kutzinski, Anna Brickhouse, Priscilla Archibald, Krista Brune, Dan Purdy, Monika Kaup, Djelal Kadir, Matthew Marr, Judith Sierra-Rivera, Susan Antebi, Ignacio Sánchez Prado, Sophia McClennen, and Laura Dassow-Wells. (North) Americanists who did agree to listen to this prying Latin Americanist were, first at the University of California Riverside, the late Emory Elliott, Katherine Kinney, and David Axelrod; then at Penn State, Sean Goudie and Hester Blum. Other times I outright tracked down and bothered strangers whose work I had read and learned from but wanted to learn more: Alan Nadel, the cultural historian of the US Cold War, humored a cold-calling stranger; the *casta* painting expert Ilona Katzew helped me track down some fugitive images. Americanists Joseph Shapiro at Southern Illinois and Matthew Garrett at Wesleyan pointed to some useful sources. The outside evaluators at the University of Virginia Press were humbling in their generosity with time and ideas, especially on how to reframe the whole thing.

The institutional support required, and received, for this kind of project is quite astounding. At Penn State, the heads of the Department of Comparative Literature, Carey Eckhardt, Robert Edwards, and Charlotte Eubanks, were encouraging and generous, and the College of the Liberal Arts was quite accommodating.

I field-tested some of the early stages of these ideas at public presentations: guest lectures at CUNY at the invitation of Araceli Tinajero, and at Pittsburgh invited by Josh Lund. Very useful feedback arose at various annual conferences of the American Comparative Literature Association and the Modern Language Association. I also learned much at gatherings held by the Society of Early Americanists in St. Augustine, the Proyecto transatlántico at Brown University, and a memorable conference on the road genre at the Universidad Nacional Autónoma de México. The "MexicanEast" research group has been putting up with my strange comparatist ideas at its yearly conferences for far too long. And, perhaps validating a usually thankless but necessary aspect of our profession, I learned quite a bit as the anonymous evaluator for tenure cases of young scholars whose names and institutions I can't divulge.

The staff at the University of Virginia Press was thoughtful, efficient, and incredibly pleasant to work with even despite a worldwide pandemic, especially Helen Chandler, Anne Hegeman, Emily Shelton, and Charley Bailey.

Finally, about twenty years' worth of graduate and undergraduate students at UC Riverside and at Penn State served as unwitting, non-IRB-approved test subjects: I hope I didn't damage them too permanently. And truth be told I wish I could name the few outright assholes who blocked the road or refused help (they know who they are for the most part) since on some fundamental level they contributed positively as well, so I thank them too.

Fellow Travelers

Introduction
Together, through the Backcountry

THE EARLY Americanist scholar Emory Elliott once said that on some level all American literature is travel literature. As a Latin Americanist, this resonated with me, because I had long held the same view about the literature I study. Latin American literature, especially during its first few centuries, is filled with explorations, encounters, lost paths, and journeys of self-discovery.[1] Although not all strictly related to travel, nearly all of it is driven by a sense of motion, of displacement through an American landscape, and it is marked by the conviction of that land's uniqueness.

The notion that the American space—both North and South—is somehow special was initially generated by a European need to celebrate the novelty and significance of the New World that had just been "found." Some form of this impulse has been constant throughout the centuries, in several historical contexts, under very different cultural and conceptual frameworks and aesthetic sensibilities. It is so ingrained that it became a cornerstone of the independent national identities across the entire continent. It is fundamental to the Latin American discourses of *americanismo* and *civilización y babarie* as well as to North American ideas of exceptionalism, manifest destiny, and rugged individualism. We might call it "geographic exceptionalism."

The chapters that follow look at three distinct historical periods of the Americas, each of which relied on conceptions of that American uniqueness as stemming from its land. Each of these periods is a historical crossroads, a moment of self-definition during which American nations were either inventing or reinventing themselves as nations. And, in order to pull that reinvention off, they looked to the land.

The first period considered is an exhilarating but chaotic time, at the end of the colonial era and beginning of the independent era, when newly emancipated nations just separated from Europe were surveying their geographic margins in order to help define what they would soon become. The second is a time of expansion during the latter part of the nineteenth century, when domestication of the frontier was an instrument of consolidation of a developing national and regional identity, and ultimately a tool of modernity. The third comes during the twentieth century, at the height of the Cold War. This was a period of entrenchment—of containment, as it were—caught in the all-consuming ideological binary at play globally. At this last moment, previous concepts of both "nation" and "empire" were forcibly reimagined, although tacitly so, by returning to the land. This book traces a fine connective thread linking these three moments in both the United States and Latin America: accounts of trips through the vast countryside. For some reason, these were of key significance at each of these historical junctures.

In the North American context, travel literature lays bare the fundamental tension between the image of the chiseled individual on the one hand, and on the other the idea of a republican collectivity, a democratic polis where everyone is represented and part of a common voice. This tension has always raised the specters of class divisions, racial and ethnic conflict, and regional prejudice and often called into question the role and function of government, both local and federal. So it stands to reason that any inventory of the national landscape—the very point of a travel narrative—often projects, and reveals, these contrasting social and political specters.

This relates to another fundamental tension that exists in both North and South, that lies deep within the formation of many national identities. It also has to do with geography, specifically with its size. It is a tension is about scale: between the intimate, the domestic, the "settled"—the personal—and the vast, panoramic, and public, in the sense of what is impossible to see all at once by any one person. It also speaks to a tension between city and country, metropolis and backcountry. As I will elaborate in more detail in the coming case studies, the backcountry (i.e., not-the-city) became essential to the metropolis, because the metropolis needs that very backcountry to define itself in contrast, and to define the entire national culture as well. Key resources for any definition of the backcountry have always been travelers' descriptions. The purpose of Hugh Henry Brackenridge's picaresque frontier-travel narrative *Modern Chivalry* (1792–1815), which is set just after American independence (and discussed in the next chapter), is, as its main character says, simply to see "what's out there."

The narratives considered here generally feature pairs of men—not an uncommon convention in travel literature. These fellow travelers, sometimes friendly and sometimes bickering, have for some reason chosen this kind of travel rather than going it alone. And when pairs are on the road, they talk. And talk. And talk.

Yet, as anyone who has taken an accompanied long road trip knows, the banter that comes up during a journey is different from ordinary talk. Perhaps it's the knowledge that the conversation is bound to be a long one and will wax and wane for an indefinite amount of time: days, months, or even years—however long the trip lasts. Or maybe it's that the talk is always secondary, never the "main thing," since the main purpose, after all, is the trip itself, and banter is only a way of passing the time, since the real goal is getting somewhere or seeing something. The imposed intimacy, contrasting with the somewhat throwaway nature of the talk, can generate a certain unscripted candor. On the road, things that probably shouldn't be said often are.

The historical period at the edge of independence, considered in the first chapter, is represented by two narratives from the late eighteenth century, Brackenridge's *Modern Chivalry* and Alonso Carrió de la Vandera's *El Lazarillo: A Guide for Blind Travelers* (1773). The first is set on the western turnpike of Pennsylvania, while the other takes place on the Royal Road between Buenos Aires and Lima. Both are lighthearted satirical works, imitations of *Don Quixote*. These road novels provide insight into how the new republics were starting to coalesce and envision themselves, and how they needed to account for their holdings. Both feature traveling agents of the state, members of the aristocratic ruling class who have set out to inventory the backcountry on behalf of the metropolis. And both of these narratives are energized by the possibility of a national constitution, as well as the promise of a new form of engineered society.

The next chapter focuses on a later period of the nineteenth century, a time of expansion into the frontier, when what had recently been immense expanses were rapidly being domesticated. An emblematic representative of this transformation is the open-range horseman, whose nomadic, quickly disappearing way of life became a master narrative for evolving national imaginations. The mythologies of both the American cowboy and the Argentine gaucho feature stoic men traveling through oceans of grass, existing freely but perilously, contending with a hostile natural environment, Indians, loneliness, and a culture of casual violence. But the real threat to their way of life comes from something else slightly farther on the horizon: the encroaching rule of law. Modernity encroaches on both the Pampas of South America and the North American West, threatening the cattle drivers with extinction. And in both cases their impending disappearance became a tragic story that was incorporated into a national mythology. The very foundational epic of the Argentine nation, the gaucho poem *Martín Fierro* published in two parts (1872–79), is the story of taming a pair of gaucho outlaws, two wanderers.

The next two chapters reflect on the complex dynamics of the Cold War, a conflict that affected North and South quite differently. "Containment culture," as the cultural historian Alan Nadel has called the prevailing ethos of the 1950s United States, was obviously quite different from what was happening in Latin America. Like the rest of the world, Latin America was caught up in the global binary of the period, wherein the United States was one of two empires pitted against each other in that conflict. During this period Latin American nations generally identified themselves with the third world, a new term that came to use during that period, holding out hope for ideological unalignment, a political "third way" (rather than economic underdevelopment, with which it later came to be associated). But, in actuality, most of Latin America could not remain unaligned, and on its own track. Its countries had to choose sides.

Despite the fact that the United States was one of the two empires in the global binary at play, and most of Latin America was at some point a proxy battlefield for it, a curious shared pattern—a kind of feedback loop—appears throughout the entire Americas during this period: stories of restless, middle-class young men who take to the road, purportedly to find the "real" America but also to escape a materially comfortable yet stifling normativity. In Jack Kerouac's *On the Road* (1957) the narrator, Sal Paradise, brimming with curiosity and yearning to be awakened, is compelled by erotic longing impossible to satisfy in his comfortable but suffocating home life. He and Dean Moriarty set out on their travels in order to find something larger than themselves but end up recreating the domesticity they left behind. Almost at the same time, another pair of middle-class young men, Ernesto "Che" Guevara and his friend Alberto Granado set out on the road. This last trip, also a trip of awakening, led to very different, if equally creative, results.

To further explore the significance of these 1950s road trips and their relationship to empire during the Cold War, chapter 4 looks at a time just after the end of the Cold War, during the 1990s, when local struggles—which for decades had been subsumed and relegated by the global binary—could now emerge on their own terms. At its height the Cold War had forced containment in the United States, a triumphalist hunkering down against an enormous and invisible enemy. Not surprising that restless young men took to the road to escape it. After its sudden end, the "road" conventions were recycled and repurposed by another traveling pair, the Mexican Zapatista leader Subcomandante Marcos and his sidekick, Durito the cartoon beetle. Marcos's "post-Marxist" virtual battlefield of the Internet gave a new place to reassemble the shards of the Cold War in a novel, yet familiar, way.

For years US scholars have been posing the questions: Do the Americas have a common history? and Do the Americas have a common literature (Lewis Hanke 13, Pérez-Firmat 21)? *Fellow Travelers* assumes that the answer to both questions is a resounding yes. Although the point of departure of this book is a fairly simple list of historical, cultural, and geographical parallels between North and South America, I look for the deeper meaning of these parallels by focusing attention on trips taken into the backcountry by pairs of men. Each of these trips is fully *American*.

As mentioned earlier, all of the trips discussed here share a specific aspect: they represent trips away from the metropolis and into one of several countrysides of the Americas. The reason behind each journeys hinges on something the countryside has to offer that is clearly different from the metropolis. That "something" is neither a given nor a constant, since the specifics are quite different during the three distinct periods being considered (the early republics, frontier expansion, and Cold War containment). But, in all of these trips away from the metropolis, the trip retains its reference to that urban center. As the environmental historian Roderick Frazier Nash puts it, during the Romantic period "appreciation of the wilderness began in the cities" (44).[2]

Fellow Travelers is deliberately not about America's tortured relationship with Europe, where America is cast as an underdeveloped reflection of its cosmopolitan source. Nor is it about European consciousness looking for itself in the New World. Much work has already been devoted to those ideas—for instance, by Antonello Gerbi (98–121). Neither is it a reprise of the aristocratic Grand Tour of travel within Europe, where the sojourners—usually wealthy young men finishing their education with a tutor—look at themselves through the multilayered history and material remnants of antiquity. The trips in *Fellow Travelers* could only happen on American landscape, North and South, at certain historical moments.

The point of departure for this book is that demographic and environmental parallels between the American hemispheres resulted in some similar cultural developments. Like similar ecological pressures that produce parallel evolution in distinct biological organisms, the United States and several Latin American countries independently experienced patterns of immigration and settlement that generated analogous cultural developments. However obvious some of these basic similarities may be, most have not been well explored or, in some cases, even documented. So we are entering new territory, so to speak, especially within the context of the "backcountry," which I present here as representing a persistently American pattern of settlement.

The notion of "backcountry" as I employ it has been articulated mostly by demographers and geographers, and more recently by some cultural historians such as Eric Hinderaker and Peter Mancall in their book *At the Edge of Empire*. They define the backcountry as a kind of evolving borderlands: "By 'Backcountry' we mean the territory that lay beyond the core settlements of mainland English colonies, and generally also beyond the control of an often weak imperial state. The Backcountry was not a fixed place; its location and meaning shifted over time" (4).

As I use the notion, the backcountry is a space that belongs to the Euro-American imagination, can be found on actual maps, and is a real place in the cultural landscape. It has developed some signs of permanence—roads, towns, some forms of livelihood—and often shows great potential for growth. But it still holds significant risks to travelers and settlers: there are the dangers of isolation, Indian attacks, unannounced or unwelcome arrivals, general lawlessness, and political and administrative instability, oftentimes proxy for crises in faraway cities that have little relevance locally.

In the backcountry, the significant distances between sparse congregations of people make communication and trade slow and often treacherous. The basic structures of order, law, and property are present but fairly thin, and so are the human relationships usually facilitated by them. Often such basic structures have to be quickly reinvented or reinterpreted, especially when settlements begin to grow and become more established. But, even when they start finding stability, the settlers and their communities remain quite different from the faraway metropolis. Within modern literary and intellectual history, an understanding of the "backcountry" as a national crucible has been in play at least since Frederick Jackson Turner's influential "frontier thesis" of 1893.

For Turner, a key function of the backcountry is that its "limit-ness"—its bordering function—reflects both the past and the future. It is also constantly evolving. For instance, while a certain wilderness (say, Pennsylvania in the eighteenth century) may have very recently been the absolute edge of the maps and of European "civilization," this absolute boundary moves on and is replaced, often quite rapidly, by the more transitional "backcountry."

For nearly two centuries in North America, this pattern played a significant role in forging a national character. Turner noticed this at the end of the nineteenth century, just as the western frontier was closing. This constant process of pushing back the geographic limit is central to Turner's assertion that US-American character traits of self-reliance, ingenuity, and material progress were a direct result of a contest with, and ultimate triumph over, an untamed land. This is the origin of the myth of American individualism, the love of open spaces, and skepticism about centralized governments trying to restrain both of those. It ultimately undergirds a very American version of modernity and the concomitant notions of democracy and political republicanism (Turner 36).

The reality, at least geographically, is more subtle. In the United States, as the geographic limit of "culture" moved beyond the Eastern Seaboard, it was slowed somewhat by several natural barriers: first the Alleghenies, then the Ohio River, the Mississippi, the interminable green seas of the Plains states, and the Rockies. But in general the progress was astonishingly swift, given the amount of difficult territory involved. This happened partly because the West was never a symmetrical or empty tabula rasa: it was intersected by veins of settlements that had sprouted up along the more accessible waterways. (The Ohio Valley and several shores of the Great Lakes were settled before western Pennsylvania.) In any case, during a relatively short period of time, and generally in a westward direction, an enormous expanse of forbidding real estate very swiftly stopped being the absolute boundary.

Once the absolute border had moved on, what remained was backcountry. It has the burning memory of having recently *been* that limit. As Turner wrote, "Within the lifetime of many living men, Wisconsin was called the 'Far West,' and Minnesota was a land of the Indian and the fur traders, a wilderness of forest and prairie beyond the 'edge of cultivation'" (341). From the second half of the nineteenth century through the middle of the twentieth, we find numerous narratives recalling true and dangerous wilderness before the advent of the new backcountry. Some popular instances, among many, include Laura Ingalls Wilder's *Little House* novels, set in the 1870s and 1880s (but not published until the 1930s and 1940s), and Frederick Russell Burnham's *Scouting on Two Continents* (1926). These books tell of a childhood during which encounters with dangerous animals, general lawlessness, and even Indian attacks were still real possibilities—in Wisconsin and Indiana! But these stories are told from a subdued present, idealizing that now-disappeared time of wildness, and, when they do relate those dangers and challenges, they form stories of an exemplary struggle simply to grow up.³ The domestication of the landscape within the recent past is part of the phenomenon Richard Slotkin studied so comprehensively in his *Frontier* books. It also resonates with the concept of "unsettlement," as articulated in the writings of Wendell Berry and more recently by Anna Brickhouse, who observes the function of "unsettlement" just before the formation of modern American nation-states (2, 293n29).

The relatively fast disappearance of a certain way of life tied to the land has a Latin American analogue. It is less stark. Rather than wilderness being replaced by "cultivation" (which had largely happened in Latin America centuries earlier), what is happening there is more an agrarianism being lost to a settled modernity, perhaps closer in spirit to what was seen in white southern US culture after the Civil War. As a cultural formation, this Latin American literary and artistic theme is known variously as "the telluric," or *criollismo*. It features many *novelas de la tierra,* or "novels of the land." Full of nostalgia and regional color, its stock settings were the rural areas existing at something similar to Jackson Turner's "edge of cultivation" (43). Signature works include Ricardo Güiraldes's novel *Don Segundo Sombra* (1926), about the last vestiges of the Argentine gaucho; Rómulo Gallegos's *Doña Bárbara* (1929), about landowners hanging onto the old ways in Venezuela; and *The Vortex* (1924), by the Colombian José Eustasio Rivera.

Clearly the cultures of North and South America have both dealt with an idealized rural locus functioning as a borderland, whose people are defined by the marginality of that borderland. While the differences are many, there are also significant and telling parallels to explore. To approach these parallels between the shifting internal borders within both Latin America and the United States, there exists some useful work on cultural geography about the edge, and limits per se—for instance, by comparative historian Felipe Fernández Armesto (149). But little work exists exploring the *transition* into backcountry. This said, the complex details of territorial expansion during the nineteenth century reach far beyond the scope of this book, especially considered in tandem with the consolidation of the national identities of the many—and quite different—geographies at hand. The United States, just by itself, spans six time zones and all five Köppen climate categories. Latin America extends from the Antarctic tip of South America northward through the high Andes, grasslands, deserts, jungles, the fertile Atlantic basins, the coasts and islands of the Caribbean, the high plains of Mesoamerica, and arguably parts of the American Southwest. We need to refer to nineteen separate

Spanish-speaking republics, each with a distinctive ecology and climate, not to mention individual political and demographic trajectories and economic destinies.

A backcountry did not emerge uniformly in all of these places. Nonetheless, a persistent and continent-wide pattern of expansive settlement *is* discernible especially in regions (including in the United States) that shared key commonalities: in terms of political organization, a strong and centralizing federalism that was heavily focused on the populous, well-established, urban political centers—that is, the cities; a vast, resource-rich countryside that was underpopulated in comparison to these cities; an aggressive (over)reach by that metropolis into that countryside as an exploitable resource to benefit itself; and, most important, an active, collective awareness of that incursive reach and the profound changes it would bring quite quickly.

By the time of Latin America's independence(s), many of its expanding and Europeanizing urban centers—such as Mexico City and Cusco—had already existed for centuries as established metropoles. New European-style cities had been overlaid onto a preexisting infrastructure of complex pre-Columbian empires, in turn already heavy with their own histories. But, upon Spanish colonization, the contrast between the cities and the less-populated *provincias* gathered new significance.

Almost invariably the provincias were perceived as semiwild areas that needed to be domesticated and made to serve the quickly growing cities. The function of the countryside was to provide the necessary raw materials: minerals, precious metals, livestock, crops, labor—anything to nourish the growing metropoles. As was the case with westward expansionism in the United States, the population of the provincias also increased, if at a slower pace and scale, as the cities themselves grew and sent out waves of internal migration. But it changed the place profoundly. As new settlers arrived, more of the absolute wilderness became transitional backcountry and pushed the true frontier farther and farther away.

During the period when nascent Latin American nations were defining themselves, from about 1810 to 1915, the division between the metropolis and the backward provincias is arguably *the* defining binary in Latin America. This opposition between "civilization and barbarism" was most notably emblematized by the Argentine statesman and writer Domingo Faustino Sarmiento in his caustic, complex portrait of a frontier warlord, *Facundo: Civilization and Barbarism* (1845). Countless political, social, economic, and cultural frictions occurred along this fault line, which ran the entirety of the nineteenth century (and beyond). Indeed, the binary continues to define much of modern Latin America; many contemporary political, demographic, and racial problems are the result of the gaping inequality between cities and noncities, a direct descendant of that old split that deepened during the nineteenth century. As the Cuban poet and revolutionary José Martí expresses in his famous 1891 essay "Our America," Latin America was "exhausted by the senseless struggle between the book and the lance, between reason and the processional candle, between the city and the country, weary of the impossible rule of rival urban clans over the natural nation, by turns tempestuous or inert" (91).

In much of the colonial Spanish American empire, as well as its successor states of independent Latin America, one of the first symptoms of encroachment came when the backcountry was vascularized by roads. These began to traverse several deserts—notably in Argentina, Mexico, and Chile. Long and arduous highways, *caminos reales,* ran along mountainous chains such as the Andes or western Mexico's Sierra Madre, arteries that retraced ancient Inca and Aztec paths. The roads connected the main, faraway cities with fertile highland valleys and coastal and lowland fishing towns. The 250-mile road from Mexico City/Tenochtitlán to the Gulf Coast was initially an Aztec thoroughfare where in just twenty-eight hours skilled runners climbed to an elevation of 7,300 feet to deliver fresh ocean seafood. There are several important rivers-as-roads—the Paraná, the Orinoco, the Balsas, the Bravo. In North America, among the better-known of those roads and rivers included the Great Wagon Road out of Philadelphia, the post roads of Boston and Albany, the Patowmack Canal, the Erie Canal, the entire Ohio Valley, and the Mississippi. All of these thoroughfares linked cities and ports to the growing backcountry settlements.

Mark Twain's descriptions of life on the river settlements blossoming along these byways show towns defined by their difference from the faraway centers. It is their remoteness that makes those settlements picturesque. St. Petersburg, Missouri, is specifically *not* St. Louis or New Orleans, its citizens colorful provincials with their own language and habits, which is part of the allure. This is very much like Gabriel García Márquez's Faulknerian Colombian province of Macondo, hacked out of the jungle on the Caribbean coast and definitely not Bogotá or even Cartagena. These are the emblematic places of a fluid backcountry whose origin myths are of recent memory.

Given its resolute distance and difference from the metropolis, the backcountry is sometimes a place of resistance toward the city and its values—sometimes of outright insurrection. As the Brazilian military engineer Euclides da Cunha describes in his eerie *Rebellion in the Backlands*

(1902), the backcountry is a place where, when an invisible and faraway central government imposes its arbitrary and paternalistic will—and its oversight—from a faraway center of power, this can naturally lead to uprisings, just like the Whiskey Rebellion in the United States right after independence. But most often the relationship between a faraway government and the backcountry is, if not necessarily friendly, one of mutual need. These two opposing cultural and geographic poles *rely* on each other to build and maintain their respective identities.

In terms of cultural production, this recalls a dynamic that occurred at a much larger scale. The Cuban writer José Lezama Lima has written about a transatlantic aesthetic, the Baroque, an urban and urbane European sensibility that also flowered in the American colonies. Addressing the *Barroco de Indias*, the New World version of the Baroque, Lezama refers to the notion of *contraconquista,* or "counterconquest." Indigenous and African American artisans and architects such as the Peruvian José Kondori and the Brazilian Antônio Francisco Lisboa (known as "Alejadinho") took possession of, and restyled, the European sensibility emanating from the centers of power. When it reached rural places, it took fantastic forms as can be seen in the folk, "Indigenous Baroque" churches of Mexico. And, as Lois Parkinson Zamora has powerfully argued in *The Inordinate Eye* (2006), it went further: when this nativized aesthetic cycled back to Europe, it created a subversive feedback loop that affected—and enriched—the source.

The underpopulated backcountry is often a place where many of the arguments and internal divisions of the metropolis are reflected and sometimes even settled. Some of the city's seemingly intractable divisions and problems sort themselves out there in ways that cannot happen in the city itself. Da Cunha defines the backlands as a place where unruly things happen that cannot (yet) happen in the metropolis, but that prefigure the future of the nation: miscegenation, free-form religious syncretism, individual rights (42).

I am signaling a reality of the postindependence American backcountries, both North and South: that they contain a referential triangularity. Within the relationship of metropolis to countryside, there is always a third point at play. All of the American metropoles—the Philadelphias, Limas, Charlestons, and Buenos Aireses—exist in complicated relationships with their respective European mother countries, Spain and Britain. These American cities know what it is to have been secondary backcountries. During the colonial period, the nexus between the American metropoles and their own *provincias* developed as a reflection of, or sometimes in concert with, the metropoles' diminishing power with respect to the European mother countries. Despite efforts toward cultural and psychic independence, and much energy spent to make American cities and capitals the true centers of the new nations, Europe loomed large. The newly independent American centers of power were always already belated, affected by the sting of separation from their origins. Buenos Aires will never be Paris, and Colonial Williamsburg will never be Mayfair. This constant reminder tinged American cities' relationship with their own rural backcountries, their own internal colonies (the great "Western Reserve" in the wilds of Ohio was initially a colony of . . . the colony of Connecticut).

In the early republics, the American metropoles' relationship to Europe was superimposed onto the backcountry in ways that mimicked or even repeated the European project of empire. In a few instances, the backcountry managed to resist this faraway central authority. Again, recall the Whiskey Rebellion and several slave and indigenous uprisings, and perhaps even the US Civil War. It would be too broad a claim to argue that this pattern existed in all of the nations under discussion, since they developed their own distinct and quite strong identities, with separate relationships to the European mother countries and distinct patterns of immigration. But, even as the relationship between the new American nations and their mother countries dissipated in the wake of independence, this same kind of relationship continued in the links between the metropoles and their own backcountries. Something did remain constant: the American backcountry was, and always would remain, not-the-city. And sometimes both ends of empire—the mother country as well as the backcountry—served to remind the American metropoles of *what they are not*.

In two quite similar speeches written just ten years apart (1837, 1847), Ralph Waldo Emerson and South American founding father Andrés Bello would declare to academic audiences who and what an "American scholar" should be, urging spiritual independence from Europe. Bello and Emerson, fellow travelers whose unexplored and startling parallels demand more attention, take a similar Romantic line about the importance of subjectivity: how human beings regard their natural surroundings. Emerson proclaimed that the American thinker, in order to learn any truth about himself, must first know his local environment (335). And, in order to establish that knowledge, the individual must be practical, assertive, and independent, and must overcome a handicap: "We have listened too long to the courtly muses of Europe," according to Emerson, an outward-looking and self-distancing habit that has made Americans timid. Bello, in a speech commemorating the tenth year of the University of Chile, furthers this exact sentiment: "Shall we search about the hygiene and pathology of the Chilean man in European books, and not study to what extent the organization of the human body is modified by the climactic accidents of Chile, Chilean customs? . . . This holds for mineralogy, geology, the theory of meteors, heat theory, the theory of magnetism; the basis of all these studies is the observation, local observation, everyday observation, observation of natural agents" (288–89).[4]

Only when "local observation" is able to address what is truly American—which even pathology and physics can uniquely be—will true self-definition happen. All the elements of "Americanness" seem to hinge on the immediate eye of the beholder. Both Bello and Emerson argue that all that is American, from the vast landscape to the smallest intricacies of human physiology, will only come into focus via the will of an observing "I." Any overarching American sense of self will only come into its own through a specific act of subjectivity. The perceiving eye needs to be close to the physical sources, the environment, the immediate surroundings—the landscape.

Of course, there is no single American physical environment on which to base a New World sensibility; the specifics vary wildly. But it is useful to speak of a backcountry-"ness." Whatever the historical, territorial, or ecological particularities, the concept of backcountry became a common and crucial tool, and part of the process of building the metropolis's sense of itself (wherever *that* was heading). Trips and expeditions for experiencing what's out there are key to defining this backcountry-ness—and, by extension, American-ness. The following chapters point to this insistent practice throughout the intellectual life of the Americas, especially during moments of national invention and consolidation. It is no coincidence, as historian Bill Hubbard notes in a book on the history of the "grid" method of mapping the early United States, that three of the four presidents carved into Mount Rushmore had been wilderness surveyors (ix). They served at times when the nation needed its backcountry the most.

The continental United States covers three million square miles, Latin America eight million. For much of its recorded human history, this terrain was either underpopulated or inhabited by a native population with a Stone Age technology that seemed to European interlopers to be part of the natural landscape, no matter how complex or densely populated the cities. This is why many of the European origin narratives, from both ends of the continent, are by and about explorers who ventured into the wilds; often these are tales of hardship and deprivation. The early literary histories of the Americas are full of harrowing chronicles of hunger, abduction, and cannibalism, of dire encounters with Indians, outlaws, and pirates. There are memoirs by hermits and missionaries, shipwreck tales, stories of captivity and escape, and Robinsonades. In this vein we could sketch a line extending from Cabeza de Vaca's *Narrative* (1542) through John Smith's *Generall Historie of Virginia* (1624) all the way to Gabriel García Márquez's *The Story of a Shipwrecked Sailor* (1970) and Jon Krakauer's *Into the Wild* (1996), with many, many similar stops in between.

I must reemphasize that the notion of backcountry on which I am relying is *not* the untamed wilderness, or the absolute desert. It is a transitional space, if one that has inherited some of the cultural valence of that original notion of "wilderness." Biologists refer to an "ecotone" as the transitional space between biomes, where there are still elements of both. The backcountry is still plenty wild, even if it is now mostly tamed.

For millennia of Western culture, the wilderness was where hardy souls retreated to isolate themselves from society, seek astringent hardships that would prompt self-reflection, and hopefully induce some form of conversion or transformation. A traditional function of the true wilderness is to provide a place to escape. Where outlaws often hide out, it is the *inimici loco,* a hostile setting that leads travelers to genuineness and clarifying introspection. One could flee from a decadent or shallow civilization in order to find and confront true sentiment, to gain depth in the presence of one's own deep solitude. Traveling to and through the wilds meant a risky internal journey of body and soul, a trip of geographic discovery as a trip of self-discovery. The wilderness was the place of askesis (ἄσκησις), an intentional privation in which loneliness and hardship made self-discipline necessary—hence the word "asceticism."

Simon of the Desert (1965), a film made by the Spanish filmmaker Luis Buñuel during his exile in Mexico, tells the story of the fourth-century ascetic hermit Simeon Stylites (AD 388–459). Simon withdrew into the Syrian wilderness, placing himself in great physical extremes for years: he stood on top of a pillar in order to become closer to God. In Buñuel's film, Simon fends off hunger, the elements, and temptation from the Devil (played by the telenovela temptress Silvia Pinal). In one hilarious moment Simon decides that standing alone on his pillar does not provide him quite enough hardship. He looks around for a way of depriving himself even more—and lifts a leg. He stands on one single leg for the rest of his life.

Placing oneself "out there" into the extreme, for the purpose of self-improvement, is squarely behind the myth of American individualism and self-reliance.[5] This is the same self-denying and self-reliant impulse that Henry David Thoreau feigns in *Walden* (1854); his "remote" cabin was actually in the suburbs and near enough for an occasional Sunday dinner at home. The thinking is that reducing the self to the minimal elements required to survive in the hinterlands will lead to resourcefulness, self-containment, and technological ingenuity—and to an revelation of what one truly "is." As an added benefit, if the traveler survives the ordeal, he or she will have a great story to tell upon returning. Sharing that harrowing tale, the storyteller is often taken as an exemplar of what is possible only for those who are hardy enough. Travelers learning about what is out there learn about the beauty and harshness of the land, but, more important, they learn about themselves when they engage with, and survive in, that land.[6]

This spirit is at the center of a work found at the beginnings of both Latin American and US literary histories. Alvar Núñez Cabeza de Vaca's *Narrative* (1542), a story of survival in the wilderness, became a sensation in Europe and was reprinted many times. The *Narrative* is the official report by the last survivor of an ill-fated Spanish expedition, launched from Cuba into Florida in the hope of finding the next city of gold, like the one recently conquered in Mexico. However, the expedition quickly foundered and ran into a series of increasingly awful disasters. The tale degrades from an epic quest for gold into a survivor's tale in which the narrator and his shrinking band exist at the edge of starvation. They end up traveling several thousand miles through absolute wilderness, on foot and in makeshift boats, from the coast of Florida to what is now the American Southwest over the course of nine years, between 1527 and 1536.

Cabeza de Vaca wrote the narrative from memory as an excuse for the expedition's failure, and as such it bears the marks of a legal/notarial genre addressed to the authorities, a *relación*. Such documents were after-action reports meant either to make sure recognition and rewards went to those who deserved them, or to assign blame. The *Narrative* is full of the required formal conventions and facts, along with some fantastic and highly entertaining finger-pointing and self-aggrandizement.

Cabeza de Vaca's expedition in search of treasure quickly becomes a desperate search for something to eat, to the point that some of the Spaniards resort to cannibalism and scandalize the natives. As several critics have pointed out, this narrative, initially committed to a quest for gold, transforms itself into a quest for another commodity valuable to the metropolis: an intelligence report about what's exploitable, what is out there. This transformation also marks the passage from legal document into the realm of literature. The *Narrative* includes astonishing epic and biblical elements wildly out of place in such a matter-of-fact legal deposition: resurrections, burning bushes in the desert, androgynous demihumans who perform evil miracles, subsistence on edible dirt. The story of conquest reinvents itself into a story of reinvention. It is a shrewd and well-crafted conversion narrative. Survival becomes the ultimate prize, something that would be impossible without the deep ontological and moral reinvention of the main character.

The high point of *Narrative* comes when the protagonists have reached what surely looks like the last straw—yet another disaster at sea, when the party sets out on some boats they had improvised:

> And it was necessary for us to undress and endure great labor in order to launch. . . . And thus embarked, at a distance of two crossbow shots out to sea, we were hit by such a huge wave that we were all soaked, and since we went naked and the cold was very great, we dropped the oars from our hands. And with a successive wave the sea overturned our raft. . . . Those of us who escaped naked as the day we were born and [we had] lost everything we carried with us. . . . [It was] November and the cold very great, we, so thin that with little difficulty our bones could be counted, appeared like the figure of death itself. For myself I can say that since the month of May I had not eaten any other thing but toasted maize. . . . The Indians. . ., when they saw us in this manner . . . in such a strange state, they were so frightened that they withdrew. I ran after them and called them, and they came back very frightened. . . . Three members of our company had drowned. . . . [The Indians] saw two dead men, and those of us who remained were traveling that same road. The Indians, on seeing the disaster that had befallen us and the disaster that was upon us with so much misfortune and misery, sat down among us. And with the great grief and pity they felt on seeing us in such a state, they all began to weep loudly. (85–87)

Having truly lost everything they carried, and being reduced to a near-drowning, they experience a rebirth, emerging naked from the amniotic sea. Cabeza de Vaca gradually overcomes this close encounter with death to become prophet-like, an increasingly ascetic figure, having finally cast off everything he has and is. His life among the natives turns free-floating and minimal. He becomes an itinerant merchant who scurries between tribes and also serves as mediator of hostilities, since he belongs nowhere, and finally a traveling healer who gains his curative, spiritual strength when he absents himself from the admiring crowds into long periods of contemplation, abstinence, and self-denial.

The survivors finally return to Spanish "civilization" in northern Mexico. After a period of reacclimatization during which they are unable to sleep on beds or wear clothes after years of nakedness, they molt their sunburnt skin "like lizards" (349). The narrator finally makes it back to Spain and files his report. The point is that trips to the absolute edge—to wilderness at its most extreme—force conversion and transformation, and they produce great and useful stories.

This extreme ascetic formula evolves somewhat when the wilderness through which the traveler suffers is no longer completely wild but has now become backcountry. It is partly or mostly tamed, and no longer the absolute extreme. What if travelers *don't* discard absolutely everything "they carried" in the trip? What happens to the process of shedding, of transformation and conversion? What happens when the risks aren't extreme or *necessarily* fatal? This is an important gradation of the lonely trip of (self-) discovery in the solitude of absolute wilderness: pairs of travelers into the backcountry.

Men: They Just Don't Get It (Especially When It's Two of Them)

Why traveling *men*? Why not also women who traveled through the Americas, of which there are some remarkable examples (Fredrika Bremer, Fanny Calderón de la Barca) or even pairs of outlaws (Thelma and Louise)? Because, as the old truism goes, men are stupid, especially when they listen to each other. There is an old absurdist joke in Spanish about the battle of the sexes. Question: Why don't men "get it"? Answer: Because they're so busy concentrating on standing on two legs.

Men are clueless, or at least the ones we will find in the following chapters. What makes so many of them use their two legs to walk and, worse yet, talk with each other while doing so? One of the subtler points behind gender scholar Eve Kosofsky Sedgwick's concept of the "homosocial" is that the bond between two men, erotically charged or not, can be focused by an outside force beyond the grasp of either one of them—to the point that they cannot acknowledge, address, or even see it. Too often relationships between men are so weighed down by all sorts of external pressures that they fail to stand erect and recognize what's in front of their own eyes—whether that external force is true erotic love, or deep Platonic friendship, or their shared obsession for a the third element, like a woman or a shared mission. *Fellow Travelers* focuses on specific pairs of men traveling through a particular geography, men who offer a variant on Sedgwick's formulation. When men get so hermetically involved with one another—which can happen when they set out on the road together—it is even hard for them to see the landscape accurately as it scrolls by right in front of their eyes, given their close quarters and portable psychodrama. The features, promontories, and issues they run into are often arrestingly visible (especially to others), just not to them.

As pointed out by Sedgwick and other gender theorists studying British literature, one notable outside pressure on the homosocial comes from empire—a very masculine presence. Each of the cases explored in the following chapters are touched in some way by empire. And in terms of the relationship between gender and empire, an instructive detail comes from the first two centuries of colonial Mexico. During that time, empire needed to be mobile, and, likewise, its religious arm had to be ready to travel.

But men and women wanting to join religious orders faced two very different sets of choices. Women could either join the mendicant orders, such as the Discalced Carmelites, groups that ventured out and engaged with the world, or they could join cloistered orders that led them away from the world, into a life of isolated contemplation. Men, however, for many years only had one choice: the mendicants. During those first centuries of Spanish colonial rule, when indigenous pacification and conversion were crucial, men of faith needed to work in unison with soldiers, administrators, and settlers. There was little time or place for secluded hideaways where they could withdraw from the world: no Cistercian, Carthusian, or Trappist monasteries with fields, vineyards, workshops, and a life of silence and meditation. There were only Mercedarians, Franciscans, Dominicans, and Augustinians, the proselytizing orders with a mission to go "out there." This proscription was partly out of necessity: empire *needed* them to travel. Consider the massive territory that had to be Christianized under dangerous conditions. These men of the cloth ventured forth with travel as their spiritual practice. They walked and preached for God and Spain, as well as for the nourishment of their own souls.[7]

These walking priests did serve one positive, if not completely exculpatory, function: they recorded what they found. In some key cases, they managed to preserve what little remained of the native cultures destroyed by the conquerors. Part of their mission had been to reconnoiter the people and lands to be conquered, so they immersed themselves in the local cultures and languages, collecting and cataloging as much as they could; many had explicit orders of understanding the savage mind in order to defeat and assimilate it.[8] The mendicants set up a pattern of venturing into "what is out there" in order to report back to the metropolis, and those reports arguably became a template for the New World.

One or Two?

Let's consider the distinction between two specific kinds of travelers: the single traveler bent on hardship versus the pair of fellow travelers. Traveling alone is clearly the riskier proposition—even more so when the lone traveler heads to the wilderness, the wild terra incognita of both the land and the soul. He or she is more likely to have no idea what could be lurking out there, or even what the chances are of making it back. Naturally, these kinds of tales tend to be starker. By contrast, fellow travelers who venture into the semisettled backcountry are somewhat safer. Their small society of two travels to where something—but not quite everything—has been domesticated, or is in the process of becoming so. The land and the people they see there are somewhat cultivated, or at least familiar on some level. But, most important, the trips are mediated by each other's company and the knowledge that traveling by twos makes it more likely that they will return to civilization in one piece. So their trip is somewhat placated by a fair certainty of their eventual return; they can count on reporting back to the metropolis.

In his work on the academic and cultural disciplines that display the cultural Other—anthropology, ethnography, museology—intellectual historian James Clifford takes on the case of Bronislaw Malinowski (1884–1942). One of the founders of modern ethnography and a deeply cosmopolitan European man, Malinowski set out alone to the South Pacific in order to study the remote people of the Trobriand Islands. Clifford notes that Malinowski wrote two very different accounts about his travels: one, the groundbreaking ethnographic work *Argonauts of the Western Pacific*, published in 1922, and the other a personal journal that Malinowski never meant for publication but nonetheless was unearthed and published after his death.[9] The contrast between the two accounts is startling. The first work is a methodological and theoretical inquiry, whereas the second is a disturbing personal chronicle of a traveler's dark internal life in the boondocks. The journal reveals a deeply unhappy, slowly unraveling man who harbors a real hatred for the natives he was supposed to be studying dispassionately or even sympathetically. But he especially resents the isolation and the distance from home.

In the private journal we learn just how much Malinowski is vexed by his absence from the metropolis, from the cities of Europe, as well as by his enforced celibacy. He relies heavily on injected drugs to hold himself together. He is clearly at the edge on many counts. Finding himself at the "furthest point of navigation" and as far away from civilization as is humanly possible, his entire sense of self is on the verge of dissolution, as Clifford notes (102): "My whole ethics is based on the fundamental instinct of unified personality" (Malinowski 296–97). Yet he remains hopeful that putting himself at such personal risk will be justified by his monumental contribution to ethnography, and the recognition it will bring.[10] The two competing records of the trip—the double bookkeeping of sorts—reveal a single traveler becoming his own interlocutor, inventing an internal fellow traveler; it is a conversation with himself. He generates an accompanying if contradictory voice to dialogue with his traveling self as part of a desperate strategy to keep himself and his project from disintegrating.

Another poignant example illustrating what happens when a traveler is forced into solitary travel (in this case by losing his habitual travel partner) comes from the most famous pair of travelers of the early US republic, Lewis and Clark. On October 10, 1813, several years after the conclusion of their famous journey across the continent, Meriwether Lewis—now governor of the Louisiana Territory—was traveling alone along the Natchez Trace to Washington, DC. He stopped at an inn, and, late that night, alone in his room, he shot himself. Some suspected murder, but the reality is that Lewis had plenty of reasons to fall prey to the dark shadows of despair.[11] He'd recently failed at a courtship, had serious personal financial difficulties, and was fighting serious allegations of administrative mismanagement. He was on his way to Washington to try to clear his name.

Lewis had a lifelong history of melancholia, a mental state exacerbated by solitary travel. A record of his depression is coded into the remarkable journals of the expedition with Clark. The most widely available modern edition, assembled by literary historian Bernard de Voto (1953), combines selections from both men into a single narrative. But, as several readers have noted, there's an imbalance between the two voices: for entire days, even weeks, Lewis falls silent. During those silences, Clark's words fill the void. He seems to take over, maintaining the orderly flow of dates, places, and scientific observations. In a historical study of suicide, psychologist Kay Redfield Jamison argues that this points to the times when fellow travelers had to carry Lewis, literally and narratively, in order to keep both the expedition and the story moving. When Lewis shut down, his fellow traveler Clark was there to cover for him.

Displacement—any form of travel—comes with heightened and inherent risks: unreliable transportation, bad roads, weather, unfriendly encounters, criminals seeing an opportunity in the strangers, hunger, running out of basics, and just plain getting lost. The critic Emily Apter has wryly noted that, in the uncomfortable decontextualization of modern travel, even boredom can become threatening (7). But some of the biggest dangers come from within. There is a strong tradition of voyagers who go into the wilderness and put themselves in harm's way as a way of reaching introspection. But this urge makes it somewhat difficult to consider a related, but less extreme, form of venturing out: instead of lonely pathbreakers going into the dangerous wilderness, fellow travelers heading into the backlands. When journeying through any sort of unfamiliar territory, introspection and self-doubt can overtake the traveler; for someone like Lewis, this can end in dangerous despair. Lewis's suicide on his final journey was arguably due to the fact that this time he was alone. After having been on the trail for so long with a fellow traveler on whom he could rely, the absence proved fatal. That night Clark was not there to cover for him.

The cases of Malinowski and Lewis both point to the increased risk of solitary travel. The traveler has to watch out to keep from falling into solipsism. Traveling with someone else and being engaged in a running conversation can also carry problems, but ultimately the trekker's dictum points to the safer choice: never go out alone. Share. Help each other stay on track. It can be dangerous not to do so.

Worth noting is the fate of Lewis's story itself. At the end of his life, another problem that weighed on him was a serious case of writer's block. He'd been pestered for years by everyone from his publisher to Thomas Jefferson, who wrote to him that the "world was anxiously expecting" his papers. The night he killed himself, Lewis had with him the journals that he'd been working on for far too long. It took another fellow traveler—the tireless editor and curator, the devoted de Voto—to make sure that Lewis would be able to finish his trip, and his story, more than a century later.

A Sense of an Ending

> "True," said the commissary, "for he has himself written his story as grand as you please, and has left the book in the prison in pawn for two hundred *reals*."
>
> "And I mean to take it out of pawn," said Ginés, "though it were in for two hundred ducats."
>
> "Is it so good?" said Don Quixote.
>
> "So good is it," replied Ginés, "that a fig for 'Lazarillo de Tormes,' and all of that kind that have been written, or shall be written

> compared with it: all I will say about it is that it deals with facts, and facts so neat and diverting that no lies could match them."
> "And how is the book entitled?" asked Don Quixote.
> "The 'Life of Ginés de Pasamonte,'" replied the subject of it.
> "And is it finished?" asked Don Quixote.
> "How can it be finished," said the other, "when my life is not yet finished?"
>
> —Cervantes, *Don Quixote*

So, on what terms do fellows travel together? The political overtones of the phrase "fellow traveler" harken to a certain kind of collaborator, a sympathizer or reliable ally who can be counted upon, but is not necessarily a card-carrying fighter fully committed to the cause. In the words of Leon Trotsky, "As regards a 'fellow-traveller,' the question always comes up—how far will he go? This question cannot be answered in advance, not even approximately. The solution of it depends not so much on the personal qualities of this or that 'fellow-traveller,' but mainly on the objective trend of things" (14). The "personal qualities"—the individual's level of commitment—only matter to the degree that he or she can contribute to the enterprise as a whole, the "objective trend of things." This is an interesting standard if applied to the fellow travelers considered in this book, who are quite often agents of a larger enterprise—the metropolis and/or empire, for instance—but whose ultimate loyalty, at least during the trip, is really to one another. When the pair is out there, they answer only to each other. They are out there alone, and reconnection (and the report) to the metropolis from which they set off at their own risk will only come later. On whose behalf are they out there—their own, or the before-and-after metropolis? How far will they go for either of these?

Another way of thinking about this is to compare the kinds of reports made by the individual traveler with those of the traveling pair. What the single traveler sees is quite different from what the pair sees, and the reasons compelling each type of observation are often also quite different. One could argue that the lonely traveler, who is out for and by himself, carries a heavier burden. During the eighteenth century, picaresque tales (as I will discuss in more detail in the following chapter) are often stories of escape, of displacement, in order to avoid either an unbearable situation or an inevitable future. Think of Daniel Defoe's *Robinson Crusoe* (1719), in which the main character is constantly fleeing a loathed, bourgeois "middle station" where he would have landed had he remained in England. Ironically, when he is marooned on his island, Crusoe builds for himself a version of this same middle station, alone on his little estate/compound, becoming a gentleman farmer who hunts and is attended by his manservant, Friday. He even painstakingly manufactures a wooden board just to have a shelf on which to display his possessions. Similarly, in Cabeza de Vaca's *Narrative* there is a sense of inescapable predestination. Upon his return to Spain years later, the narrator learns that a soothsaying Moorish woman had predicted the disastrous failure of the expedition before it started (174).

Traveling to escape, or to alter oneself and the course of one's inevitable future, are quite different from traveling to see what's out there, with the explicit intention of coming back, with a report in hand. The first involves traveling to survive, whereas the second means surviving the travel. Both rely on truth claims but in different ways. Literary historian Roberto Gonzalez Echevarría has argued that the origins of modern Latin American literature lie not in traditional forms and genres such as poetry, drama, fiction, or essays, but rather in evidentiary discourses. The true foundations can be found in the law, scientific reportage, and journalism, and later on in anthropology (56). Indeed, in Latin America there is a strong tradition of *letrados*—men (with a few notable female exceptions) trained as lawyers, colonial administrators, and bureaucrats—who would become the intellectual marrow of the learned culture.[12] Given their primary occupations as fact-purveyors, it was natural that when they turned to more creative endeavors a chief literary concern was veracity, some form of truth claim.

Many Latin American travel narratives (and there are many), even farfetched ones, fall solidly within in this tradition. Many survivors' tales, like some of the survivors themselves, find that they are reduced to skin and bones, to the minimal elements. This diminution gives impressive credence to the stories, made more powerful because of their very gauntness. Emaciation bears witness of hardship and hunger, lending credibility; the body in distress offers evidence and serves as proof of the veracity of an account.

Another frequent element of these truthful travel narratives is their positive outcome, their happy ending: the protagonist has made it back. And, having returned, the survivor is somehow better off by being able to tell about it. Oftentimes what kept the traveler going was the burning *nostos*, the desire to come home, and to deliver a startling report of the trip. As the Spanish saying goes (also the title of Gabriel García Márquez's memoir), *vivir para contarla*—live to tell the tale. And, as literary critic Frank Kermode long ago pointed out in *The Sense of an Ending* (1967), the certainty that the story will ultimately come to an end gives shape to that story as it is developing and gives form to its entire arc.

This said, there are clearly degrees of intensity in traveling, and variations in the kinds of stories. Travelers whose safe return is highly uncertain (e.g., conflict survivors, exiles, refugees, and migrants) usually tell stories energized by perils and the sheer unlikelihood of success. The stories I have gathered here deliberately are not this extreme. For the most part, the travelers in these stories have set out with a reasonable expectation of returning to their home environment—an important formal distinction to both the trips and the stories they produce. When a journey is predicated on an eventual debriefing, the trip has somewhere to go. It is, from its outset, teleological.

These stories are also dialogic; they are predicated on pairedness. To offer a spatial metaphor, they are narrative "ecotones," a concept from earth science referring to the place where two distinct biomes meet and exchange elements—biospheric dialogue. But dialogism has a temporal aspect as well: as the Russian theorist Mikhail Bakhtin notes about dialogue, it progresses, it is also inherently end-driven. It creates a trail of signification where the expectation of a reply informs, and ultimately shapes the flow, like the trail of alternating footsteps in a long march: "The word in living conversation is directly, blatantly, oriented toward a future answer-word: it provokes an answer, anticipates it and structures itself in the answer's direction" (279).[13] When there is dialogue between travelers, open-ended wandering is still punctuated by its regularity. The larger-scale dialogism—between the travel itself and the eventual, expected return and subsequent report—are both there from the start, carried from the "home" and into the "away" and the "out there." The story—even if it does not yet exist—cannot help shaping the entire journey, as well as many of the choices made by the travelers. Travelers to extreme places always carry the weight of their home with them in some way, since they will return to it. This is Sedgwick's external mediating pressure, even if its text has yet to be written. My method in these pages reflects these pressures as I, too, go back and forth between the metropolis and the backcountry.

This is not to say that all dialogic travel narratives are preordained "done deals." But those who travel with such a driving end purpose never quite abandon the pull of its outcome. They will tell a very particular kind of story, because this kind of travel sets in place specific mental patterns. Travel in all its forms affects the subject—how can it not? But how does it transform the observing traveler whose mindset is fashioned by the prospect of his or her return? The transformative nature of travel in such cases is complicit with its ending, which is a story carried from the outset. As observers of both early North American and Latin American literature point out, the books literally carried by newcomers to the New World shaped the sights that were right in front of them as much as their own eyes did, if not more so.[14] Some baggage from home cannot be easily discarded by the side of the road.

A final consideration arises about a traveler who is an agent of empire and travels into colonial otherness. When the traveler regards what he sees with a colonizing eye—even when that traveler is compromised by the rigors of travel, broke, lost, or hungry—he is still a colonizer. What kind of cast does that put on what he sees? What the critic Mary Louise Pratt has called the "imperial eye" (176) speaks to this acquisitive impulse in travel—for instance, in the case of Alexander von Humboldt. But is it possible that the instabilities of such travelers, even if they result from self-imposed hardships, can open their vision *somewhat*? Marxist critic Antonio Cornejo Polar refers to the pushback "pressure of the referent" of the colonized "Other" upon the colonizer: Can the subaltern speak through an agent of the imperial project of observation/cataloging/conquest, if the latter is unsettled by travel (Paoli and Cornejo 259)?

A partial answer, which I will flesh out in the following chapters, is that, when the colonizing selves travel as a reduced form—the pair, the minimum required for dialogue—and talk to each other in the space of otherness, strange and perhaps unmediated visions can emerge. Even when the pair is busy engaging each other in the face of otherness, that otherness can creep into their supposedly "closed" society of two. This can happen in spite of the stupid pair. The pair of stupid travelers invokes a thread from literary history (which Bakhtin follows closely) that will surface in the following chapters. The literary picaresque features such a split between the individual and the traveling pair. The "true" original picaresque is the story of a lonely, often desperate picaro who travels under great hardship: he has no choice but to keep moving. The source of this tradition, the Spanish novel *The Life of Lazarillo de Tormes and of His Fortunes and Adversities* (1554), tells the story of a young, lowly born protagonist who moves from one misfortune to another, creating an episodic structure and a tone that gained a powerful place within the Western imaginary. This novel influenced many forms and genres, including travel literature (many scholars have argued that it is the source of the modern novel).

Yet another literary genre grew from the picaresque, but it is fundamentally different in some key aspects: the quixotic. This mode is par excellence the story of a traveling pair. It also introduces elements of delusion and stupidity and questions the reasons for embarking on a trip that is certain to run into mishaps. Don Quixote goes so crazy from reading so many adventure stories about wandering knights that he now sets out to live one of these stories himself. However, the world into which he wanders has no place for these fantastic tales or for his deluded self. The companionship of Sancho, his somewhat more perceptive but still stupid companion, only makes matters worse; they talk themselves into many, many misunderstandings and hard knocks. Whereas a canny, "true" picaresque protagonist like the lonely Lazarillo de Tormes travels to survive, the quixotic hero is sustained in his fantasy world, which keeps confirming what he believes he is—a knight on a quest—despite much evidence to the contrary. And he keeps going in his delusion, thanks in great part to his traveling companion.[15]

I return to a particular aspect of the traveling pair. These two are so caught up in their own little world that the "real" world is (mostly) ignored by them, as happens with Sancho and the Don. But, worse yet, when they *do* see it, their concerted interpretation often leads to talking each other into misunderstanding or misrepresenting what's there, to the point that they completely foul things up. This kind of interaction—a direct result of their togetherness, their traveling relationship, and their friendship—places them in a parallel existence to the world through which they are traveling, not unlike the dream-cave of Montesinos into which Don Quixote is lowered (2:22–23).[16]

This parallel existence of the Don and Sancho nonetheless reflects *something* out there. After all, for generations critics have powerfully argued that *Don Quixote* is the first "realist" novel (even if that usually refers to a realistic depiction of delusion). But is this "something out there" what they were carrying with them from before? The long-standing debate about whether or not the Don is mad or (perhaps too) sane—the so-called "soft" versus "hard" readings of the *Quixote*—is really about what to do with an insight when it comes from a deluded subject. Can a fool or a madman who is disconnected from his immediate world distill genuine and insightful knowledge about his circumstances—the classic, otherworldly "holy fool" studied by Walter Kaiser (109)? Or, if this pair is genuinely stupid and lacking any true sense of "I am myself and my circumstances," as Ortega y Gassett famously phrased it in his *Meditations on Quixote,* then what is the worth of their accidental, or *stupid,* wisdom about the "circumstances" they do not quite get (257)?

I would contend that knowledge derived from stupidity is not necessarily completely worthless or disposable. Considering stupidity as an epistemological category, philosopher Avital Ronell writes that the standard for stupidity is a counterfactual lack of self-awareness: "The stupid cannot see themselves. No mirror yet has been invented in which they might reflect themselves. They ineluctably evade reflection. No catoptrics can mirror back to them, these shallowest, most surface-bound beings, the historical disaster that they portend" (18). This assessment is especially apt for a pair of stupid travelers: the wilderness they traverse, and its more settled "backcountry" relative, are places ripe for self-discovery and self-fashioning. The stupid pair *should* be able to find themselves in the backcountry, but this is exactly what the Don and Sancho fail to do. The two are so busy engaging with each other that they fail to engage with the world around them. They cannot recognize, or participate in, how that world defines them. They never see how that world sees *them*.

What *does* their world-ignoring traveling friendship—their stupid-making "pairedness"—have to offer, if anything? And why are the stories of self-involved travelers so persistent, so recurrent? Postcolonial critic Leela Gandhi identifies the asymmetrical friendships that can sometimes grow between the colonizer and the colonized subject. Taking examples from the British Raj, she finds specific instances where a colonial traveler, a well-meaning agent of empire, goes to the subjected lands and befriends the subaltern. That friendship sometimes leads to unusual results: "If . . . I defiantly choose or 'elect' my affinities, will I escape the deadlock of self-identical community? Will my voluntary affiliations, still desperately seeking similitude (of sexual, intellectual, political, ethical, aesthetic orientation) endlessly replicate the deadlock of self-sufficient unity?"(25).

Gandhi is pointing to something that happens when subjects of unequal standing find themselves—voluntarily—traveling together in a place that is neither one's nor the other's. What she calls "philoxeny," the homosocial bond of friendship that results from traveling together, in this case is predicated on a mutual acceptance of the power imbalance. When travelers of unequal standing enter into their own parallel world, this acceptance of the difference can actually become an emancipatory act, because it casts aside the structures that would normally uphold the inequalities. While on their trip, they have cast aside their identification with a certain class or status, and because of this "[they] carry exceptional risk" (29).[17] This kind of leveling friendship calls for a novel kind of agency—a newly forged force of will and representation, in the Schopenhauerian sense, that goes *against* the demands of the world in favor of its own closeness.

The traveling companions create their own affective realm, their own little world. I will elaborate on this, especially in case studies of the gaucho and the cowboy during expansionist periods, as well as the "road" genre during the Cold War. Some traveling friendships from these periods are idealistic, as Gandhi argues, but also, in their apartness, somehow inadvertently yet deeply reflective of the world that has been left behind. The trips and the friendships are forged by the pressures that led the travelers, at least for a while, away from an imperfect world and into a little portable one.

To begin the journey I turn to a story by Jorge Luis Borges, "The Ethnographer" (1969), that breaks down the steps of traveling "out there" with the express purpose of reporting back. It tells of a young researcher, a North American named Murdock, who ventures somewhere into the wilds of the southwestern United States for fieldwork among the natives. Once he is in the wilderness, Murdock suffers many transformations and hardships, finally connecting with a shaman: "The teacher at last revealed to him the tribe's secret doctrine. One morning, without saying a word to anyone, Murdock left." Murdock returns to the metropolis that had sent him out.

> He made his way to his professor's office and told him that he knew the secret, but had resolved not to reveal it.
>
> "Are you bound by your oath?" the professor asked.
>
> "That's not the reason," Murdock replied. "I learned something out there that I can't express."
>
> "The English language may not be able to communicate it," the professor suggested.
>
> "That's not it, sir. Now that I possess the secret, I could tell it in a hundred different and even contradictory ways. I don't know how to tell you this, but the secret is beautiful, and science, our science, seems mere frivolity to me now."
>
> After a pause he added: "And anyway, the secret is not as important as the paths that led me to it. Each person has to walk those paths himself."
>
> The professor spoke coldly: "I will inform the committee of your decision. Are you planning to live among the Indians?"
>
> "No," Murdock answered. "I may not even go back to the prairie. What the men of the prairie taught me is good anywhere and for any circumstances."
>
> That was the essence of their conversation.
>
> Fred married, divorced, and is now one of the librarians at Yale.
> (*Fictions* 335)

Once he is back, he declines to convey the "secret doctrines" he has learned. The devastating, single-sentence paragraph that concludes the tale ("Fred married, divorced, and is now one of the librarians at Yale") is pure Borges. This turns the expectations of the travel genre on its ear:

the traveler returns as expected, but the motivating force behind it—the report to his home culture about what is out there—is forever postponed, not worth pursuing. Murdoch did undergo the expected, momentous transformation out there, and he learns secrets about and from the wilderness, and from the Other who inhabits it. But the real secret he has discovered is about setting out in the first place.

Murdoch abandons the excitement and challenges of traveling further and writing about it in exchange for an unremarkable existence. He ends up a librarian, a keeper of others' knowledge, rather than the searcher, collector, and revealer of his own truths. What he learned out there has made him unwilling to write his own story, to account for his own journey. The preordained formula of the return is not enough to contain or do justice to the uniqueness of his travels. Murdoch, so weighted down by the knowledge of the inevitability of return, ultimately evades it. In his librarian's obscurity there is an endless lack of finality, and, in very Borgesian fashion he finds his place—an escape from the escape, a lack of an ending.

1 Fools of Empire

A Morning Constitutional, or Blind Eyewitnesses in the Early Republics (H. H. Brackenridge's *Modern Chivalry* and Alonso Carrió de la Vandera's *A Guide for Blind Travelers*)

The "Picaresque" by the Dawn's Early Light

> He who reads much and walks much, goes far and knows much.
> —Cervantes, *Don Quixote*

The classic manual of the National Outdoor Leadership School asks a disquieting but reasonable question about choosing a campground in the dark: "Are you on the edge of a cliff that you'll forget about when you get up in the night to pee?" (Petzoldt 110). The implied lesson is simple. If you can, wait to get up until the morning, when you can see everything and stretch out your legs under the new light. It's just plain safer.

Morning constitutional: this euphemism for relieving oneself first thing in the morning offers a crude but resonant image of waking up and getting a fresh look at the lay of the land—and then marking it. This is a particularly suitable point of departure for discussing two scatological books, about two pairs of travelers who mark two territories at a new dawn. Hugh Henry Brackenridge's *Modern Chivalry, Containing the Adventures of Captain John Farrago and Teague O'Regan, His Servant* was published in a series of volumes between 1792 and 1815. The slightly earlier *El Lazarillo: A Guide For Blind Travelers* by Alonso Carrió de la Vandera was published in 1773 under the author's pseudonym, Concolorcorvo (raven-colored), the nickname of the Indian servant Calixto Bustamante who supposedly narrates the story.[1]

Both tales feature a quixotic pair of travelers—an aristocratic "Don" and a rascally squire who take to the road. And both of these funny, satirical works are connected to the beginning—the dawn—of the independent Americas. They amount to rambles at the horizons of new nations still in the process of envisioning themselves and staking their places in the world. Both books are set in the backcountry. *Modern Chivalry* takes place partly on a Pennsylvania road heading from Philadelphia to the western frontier town of Pittsburgh, which Brackenridge helped to found. *A Guide for Blind Travelers* is set on the South American Royal Road between Buenos Aires and Lima. Both are rakes' progresses modeled on the British and European comic novels then quite in vogue. Brackenridge's is more broadly comical, and closer in spirit to Rabelaisian models like Samuel Johnson's *Rasselas* or Voltaire's *Candide* (both 1759). Carrió de la Vandera's is a bit headier, and more self-referential and formally experimental, closer perhaps to Laurence Sterne's *Tristram Shandy* (1762–67). Each work weaves into the narrative useful descriptive information that contrasts sharply with the shenanigans of the main characters.

As could be expected given their quixotic source, the squabbling duos display a shadow of madness, of irrational compulsion. The mental state and abilities of both the *visitador* (or post road inspector) Don Alonso in *El Lazarillo* and Captain Farrago in *Modern Chivalry* are often called into question by their sidekicks, who complain about unreasonable demands made by their respective Dons. But there is a significant difference between the madnesses of these aristocratic travelers and that of their shared ancestor, the impoverished Spanish gentleman Don Quixote: the quests of Captain Farrago and Don Alonso are actually not all that deranged.

In *Modern Chivalry,* the reason for Farrago's quest is almost maddeningly mundane. Rather than madness from reading too many fantastic tales—as was the case for Don Quixote—what sends him on the road is simply that one day "the idea had come into his head to saddle an old horse that he had, and ride the world a little, with his man Teague at his heels, to see how things were going on here and there, and to observe human nature" (4). This is an uncomplicated wish to see, and mark, what's out there. Unlike Don Quixote's crazy reason for setting out—he's imbibed so many stories of knights fighting giants and armies that he develops the need to find them in the real world—Farrago has a much simpler and pragmatic project of surveying. His mission is visual: to *see* how "things were going on here and there."

The visual purpose behind Carrió de la Vandera's *A Guide for Blind Travelers* is announced in its title. The scurrilous narrator, the Indian Calixto, declares that he is writing for others just like him, "the people who are commonly called" the "criminal underworld" (27, my translation). Calixto will become a set of eyes for that constituency and build a detailed and practical description of the lay of the land. He will help the criminal underworld overcome its blindness, providing for its various enterprises an intelligence report of what is out there.

Clearly the announced intentions of both books run counter to the way *Don Quixote* engages with the world. It is true that all three main characters—Don Quixote, the visitador Don Alonso, and Captain Farrago—are fairly blind to what is around them, and more often than not they misunderstand what is going on. But the local observations in both *Modern Chivalry* and *A Guide for Blind Travelers* are in fact quite precise and canny, often made in the voice of a narrator who unpacks the "real" meaning of whatever the characters have just encountered but failed to see. What these books offer is both accurate and immediately valuable. They are not really blind picaresques; rather, they are travelogues in picaresque drag, if dogged by blindness. They actually oscillate between a typically quixotic utter lack of perception (which would seem normal, given the stupidity involved) and an insightful hypervision.

Here is an extended passage from *A Guide for Blind Travelers,* giving an over-the-top description of the huge carriages used to move goods and people along the road between Buenos Aires and Jujuy:

Description of a Cart

The two wheels are 2½ *varas,* more or less, in height, the center of which is a heavy hub, 2 or 3 spans wide. In the center of this is an axle of 15 spans' width on which rests the bed or box of the cart. This axle is made of a beam which is called the *pertigo,* 7 or 8 *varas* long, which is accompanied by two other beams 4½ *varas* in length, and these, when joined to the *pertigo* by four pins called *teleras,* form the box 1½ varas in width. To this structure six pointed stakes are added on each side, and between each pair is an arch made of a kind of willow wood, thus forming an arched or oval roof. The sides are covered with woven reeds, which are stronger than the cattails used by the inhabitants of Mendoza. . . . In the entire cart there is not a piece of iron or a nail because everything is made of wood. The axles and wheel naves are greased almost every day so that the hubs will not be worn away, since in these carts the axle is secured to the bed and it is only the wheel that revolves. The larger carts are no different, except that the body is made entirely of wood, like a cabin on a ship. . . .One mounts by means of a short ladder, and from the floor to the roof it measures 9 spans. The bed of the cart is covered with pampa grass or cowhide which is very smooth since it is well stretched. . . .

It is 407 road leagues from Buenos Aires to Jujuy, and the cost of shipping by oxcart is 8 *reales* per *arroba,* a price which seems incredible to anyone lacking in experience. . . .The caravans regularly stop at ten o'clock in the morning, and after a round up has been made. . . . .in these six hours, more or less, food is prepared for the people; the attendants are content with roasting, rather poorly, a sizeable piece of meat. They kill a bull if necessary and grease the wheel hubs, all of which is done with considerable speed. Some of the passengers sit in the shade of the high trees, others in the shadow cast by the cart which is extensive owing to their height. But the most sturdy and best ventilated arrangement is made when two carts are put side by side with space between large enough for another cart to fit. . . . Some carry their own small double-sawbuck stools with seats of reed or canvas. I consider the latter to be better because even if it gets wet, it is quickly dried and it is not as stiff nor as apt to split as the reed, since the attendants always pack these stools on the side of the cart, outside the box, with the result that they get wet and are often torn by the branches which protrude into the road from the low trees; wherefore, a diligent person will take the trouble to pack them inside the cart, along with a folding table which is useful for eating, reading, and writing. . . . The more energetic and curious persons ride horseback, going ahead or falling behind at their will, examining the farms and their rustic inhabitants, which are usually women, since the men go out to the fields before daybreak and do not return until they are exhausted by the heat of the sun or are ravished by hunger which they usually satisfy by eating exactly four pounds of fat and . . . meat the inhabitants called *descansada;* I call it poisoned. (90–94)

This ridiculously excessive detail, which goes on for pages, is not wrong; it is just too much. The excess is satire in the classical sense of overstuffed *satura,* leavened with some funny overelaborations, like the intricate description about where to find shade. Like *Tristram Shandy*'s ludicrous completeness about military fortifications, this sort of microscrutiny sets out to record every detail about what a traveler is likely to see on this specific stop on the trip—peasants at work in fields by the road—which in turn curlicues into even more details about the eating habits of those peasants.

Modern Chivalry, while not quite so full of curlicued details as either *Tristram Shandy* or *A Guide for Blind Travelers,* is also packed with informative anecdotes and descriptions of apparently random sights: court proceedings, the Philosophical Society, backcountry uprisings, the unscrupulous practices of Indian agents, and the meaning of the quasi-heraldic Order of the Cincinnatus. However arbitrary these may seem, they were fixtures of North American reality.

These two novels are only partly blind, because they *can see* (local) color. Both *Modern Chivalry* and *A Guide for Blind Travelers* are insightful field guides to minute, immediate environments. But there is a built-in negation, given their generic nature: the conceit of a quixotic narrative negotiates between a reality that is clearly there and a viewer— a foregrounded subjectivity—that simply does not see that reality. The reader observes the invisibility of that reality to the traveling witnesses.

When referring to the "key" perceptual structures of the eighteenth century, French philosopher and historian Michel Foucault associates blindness with travel: "What allows man to resume contact with childhood and to rediscover the permanent birth of truth is this bright, distant, open naïveté of the gaze. Hence the two great mythical experiences on which the philosophy of the eighteenth century had wished to base its beginning: the foreign spectator in an unknown country, and the man born blind restored to light" (*Birth* 65).

The relationship between the picaresque and vision relates to a critical older commonplace about the picaresque: that it is inextricably tied to empire. This idea wound its way into Benedict Anderson's *Imagined Communities* (1981). In his landmark study about the rise of modern national identity, Anderson focuses on places such as Mexico that in the early nineteenth century had only recently become independent nations. He looks at an early republic picaresque novel by journalist J. J. Fernández de Lizardi, set in Mexico City. *The Itching Parrot* (1816, published 1831) casts unique light on a time of momentous transition in Spanish America, when a certain kind of empire was being replaced by constitutionality and republicanism, which meant a new kind of national identity based on sovereignty and notions of direct democracy. Anderson argues that a related conceptual shift was happening in the sense of individual identity—a change toward the "imagined community," the idea of a simultaneous collectivity made possible by literacy, print technology, and the speed of mass media (44–45).

Anderson finds the contours of this democratic reimagination of identity by looking at its exceptions: its delinquents, like the picaro. A picaro's typical journey takes him to the undersides and margins of society, where he often falls into or clashes with the instruments meant to contain—or "discipline," in the Foucauldian sense—those margins: the military, hospitals, debtors' prisons, madhouses, religious institutions, agents of the law, indentured servitude, and many forms of con art. All of these are familiar stops (or bumps) on the typical picaro's road (Anderson 29–30). Who better to describe these than someone who has tangled with them? Critics have taken an interest in North American picaresques of this period for similar reasons. Scholar Cathy Davidson says of works such as *Modern*

Chivalry that "the picaresque novel is engaged in exploring the margins of society and not in trodding some middle way" (249).[2]

Historian Ruth Hill organizes her comprehensive look at Spanish America's Bourbon-era culture and government around what is displayed in *A Guide for Blind Travelers*. She locates Carrió de la Vandera's odd book within a popular genre of the time: functional but eclectic almanacs written in the voices of learned travelers such as natural philosophers and astrologers. These books were partly entertainment, but they also contained practical advice. Many played with the notion of blindness (*Guide for the Blind* was a common title), since astrologers and other seers held a visionary privilege over common people: they had learned to look at something ordinary and readily visible to everyone, like the heavens, and reveal a deeper meaning. Carrió de la Vandera's "exposé," as Hill calls it, "involves travel, but not exploration or exotic travel" (20). It catalogs what is generally known to exist out there but hasn't yet been organized or explained coherently or in detail: the backcountry that isn't quite "constituted."

Sightseers were crucial to the new nations. As landscape architect and historian Bill Hubbard has shown, mapping was a key step in shaping the new United States; arguably its first national-scale project was creating the "Rectangle Survey," the imaginary grid lines that cataloged the land. This monumental project registered the "public domain" of what was out there—the unsettled vastness—into often arbitrary but mathematically precise quadrangles. Hence the odd but symmetrical shapes of many states and counties that ignored the natural topography. This symmetry becomes more pronounced as the map extends westward: consider the outlines of the states of Colorado, Utah, and New Mexico. But this arbitrary grid, this structured vision overlaid onto the land, was necessary for the nation. As Hubbard notes, three of the four presidents whose portraits are on Mount Rushmore had been wilderness surveyors (9–14). They were traveler-surveyors, but also *touristes d'horizon* of the margins, in Benedict Anderson's sense. These early traveler-surveyors who went to become nation-builders shared the surveying impulse of these two quixotic novels from North and South America.

Except, of course, for the stupid part.

I'm with Stupid

Although the quixotic protagonists of these novels are patently stupid, each is stupid in his own particular way, and complementary to his traveling partner. The members of each pair are well suited to one another, not least for the cumulative comic effect or for narrative expediency. Their verbal exchanges and conflicts belie the useful information that surfaces in spite of the stupidity. Things that are serious or valuable break through despite (or even because of) the idiocy, but the seriousness can't avoid being colored by the stupidity. Sometimes it serves as a highlighting contrast, offering an entertaining counterpoint to somewhat turgid or complex issues that seem much simpler when juxtaposed with the idiots who don't "get" them—like, in *Modern Chivalry,* debates over the humanity and intelligence of "Negroes" (74–75) or the economic consequences of marriage (42–43).

This brings us to the way knowledge usually works in the quixotic genre. As mentioned earlier, at that moment in literary history (the eighteenth century) the line between the "original" picaresque and the quixotic proper had blurred in European literature. The title page of Henry Fielding's "picaresque" *Joseph Andrews* (1742) announces that, instead of being in debt to the grittier original picaresques of the *Lazarillo de Tormes* (1554) or Francisco de Quevedo's *Buscón de Alfarache* (1604), the novel is "written in Imitation of the Manner of Cervantes, Author of Don Quixote." Yet Fielding's work and many like it became known as "picaresque," and their protagonists as "picaroons." This might be considered an inconsequential slippage of a term based on a number of legitimate similarities. Or, if one wanted to expand into cultural history, one could argue that this was an effect of cultural prejudice, wherein the rest of Europe regarded Spain as an exotic, all-purpose internal Other, causing the two genres to blend tonally over time. During the seventeenth and eighteenth centuries in Europe, "Spanish stories" began to fall under the same categorical umbrella.[3]

Two obvious similarities between the two types of narrative help account for the genre trouble. First of all, both the quixotic and the original picaresque are nominally about travel, about constant motion. Second, both genres emphatically insist on truth. They chronicle goings-on that are delinquent—or borderline delinquent—so both hew close to legal discourse and its narrative forms (as the critics Roberto González Echevarría and Lennard Davis have both argued). Both proclaim their own veracity, and each is framed as some sort of evidential text, claiming to be a testimony of some sort.

The shared insistence on truth and the reliance on witnessing and visual fact calls for consideration of the difference between the two picaresque types. On the one hand, the "true" picaresque of the *Lazarillo de Tormes* is a first-person account of a boy's life, a *testimonio* told in the language such a character would likely use; the narrator sounds like a low-born scoundrel. This type of character is also often desperate, and fully aware of his own reasons for speaking, the rhetorical necessity behind his reach for words: the story is usually framed as a formal petition, a plea addressed to a higher authority who holds over him some kind of decision-making power. We hear this in the notarial-sounding first words of the *Lazarillo de Tormes:* "*Your Grace should know* before all else that my name is Lázaro de Tormes, son of Tomé González and Antoña Pérez, natives of Tejares, a small village in Salamanca" (5, my emphasis). This is a request for leniency, mimicking the sound of a deposition, in which the main evidence in his case is his hard life story. The bluntness and honesty of this rhetorical conceit is what made the genre powerful, but this simplicity also made it easily imitable, explaining why this voice embedded itself in Western literature for centuries. Just in North America, examples include *Huckleberry Finn, The Adventures of Augie March, Jesus' Son* (discussed in the last chapter), and countless other realist texts in between and since.

On the other hand is the patently *ironic* protestation of truth on the part of the narrator in *Don Quixote*. Although this novel's shape is clearly related to—and descended from—the earlier *Lazarillo de Tormes,* the truth claims in *Don Quixote* are much more complex. The world-weary narrator is a bookish witness, not the semiliterate first-person survivor of works like the *Lazarillo*. This narrator outlandishly swears he discovered his tale in the work of the "Arab historian" Cide Hamete Benengeli, whose loose pages he had found not in a library or a vault but rather in the trash of the market in Toledo (1:8–9). But this narrator, like the narrator of the *Lazarillo*, insists at great pains that this is *not* a put-on, continually professing the "veracity" of such obviously fake-news sources. His self-aware, house-of-mirrors protestations are playful and self-referential in a way that the *Lazarillo* could never be.[4]

Don Quixote's ironic relationship with truth claims stands in sharp contrast with the sincere first-person voice of the original picaresque, signaling two radically different worldviews. Yet somehow these contrasting views have become bound together by the eighteenth century: the stoic survivor of a harsh world dispassionately recording what he sees versus the pair stumbling cluelessly through that same harsh world, their failure to see generating great comic effect as highlighted by an external observer.

The nature of the protagonists is different as well. The wary solo traveler travels light, as opposed to the traveling pair, who constantly talk to each other and display their accumulated baggage, metaphorical and otherwise, noisily clanking along in their armor. It is no surprise that these two types of travelers engage differently with the world. The original picaro is fundamentally a lonely, diminished creature, traveling by and for himself, who sees everything mostly because he has to. The mad Don Quixote, by contrast, is always accompanied, and he and his story are rarely left alone; there are constant intrusions. The Don would not be the same without his sidekick and their shared shenanigans—the Don is most lost when Sancho is somewhere else. Sancho and the Don are a pair in a fundamental way: they move through the world as a pair and suffer their hard knocks together. Their resulting debates and arguments are key to their ontology, since they often talk themselves into an explanation or excuse for what has just happened to them and what they have just misunderstood—a misunderstanding that has landed them in a pickle. The two are necessary for the irony. In contrast, the true picaro will always be an existential and exactingly vigilant loner. His makeup is unironic and stark. The quixotic pair, despite—or, most likely, because of—one another's company, will always have trouble seeing straight.

The eighteenth-century blending of these two genres points to a broader question about the veracity of travelers' reports. When the true picaresque (the canny, lonely rogue's tale) becomes generically confused with the quixotic (the tale of the mythically loony and bickering pair that is full of undermining meanings), does this reveal something about what and how travelers see and report back, and their reasons for having set out in the first place? To see, or not to see?

Tell Me What You Saw on Your Trip

> I am a fish between two waters, that is, neither as ponderous as the first group nor of as little weight as the second.
> —Calixto the narrator, *A Guide for Blind Travelers*

At the beginning of *A Guide for Blind Travelers,* the sidekick/narrator Calixto Bustamante sits at his desk to write his prologue and lays out his own reasons for setting out on the trip with Don Alonso. Suddenly, his master, the postal inspector—Don Alonso Carrió de la Vandera (1715–1783), a historically verifiable figure: an actual roads inspector and the real author of the book—enters the room. The Don takes one look at what the Indian has put down on the page and begins a harangue. This happens in "real time," because Calixto quickly transcribes the argument as it happens. Don Alonso issues condescending commentary, even attempting bad verse to do so—"The architect lacks in ability / If the portico larger than the building be" (42). The Don ultimately compels the poor Indian to put "the pen in the inkwell, and the inkwell in the corner of my room, until another trip presents itself" (42). This sets the stage for the running repartee between master and servant that will motivate the entire book, about who has the upper hand, who controls words about their lengthy trip.

The framing conceit of *Modern Chivalry* displays just such a battle for the verbal upper hand, but in this case there are three rather than two competing voices: the pompous Captain Farrago, a deluded old patrician Quixote figure; his Irish footman Teague O'Regan, who is selfish, carnal, and ignorant; and the editorializing narrator, who concludes each funny episode with an epilogue unpacking the deeper meaning of what has just transpired. Not surprisingly, these competing voices have led to competing critical interpretations. The pattern seems to be that, when a critic argues that the most prominent voice is that of the Irishman Teague, the novel should be read as a protoemancipatory text, whose voice is the common man's (objectionable as he may be): a projection of liberal-democratic, Jeffersonian ideas about equality (see Looby, *Voicing* 203–65). In contrast, if the voice of either the aristocratic Captain Farrago or the editorializing narrator is heard most loudly, the text is considered Federalist and Hamiltonian (see Shapiro). And some critics—including Ed White, editor of the most recent scholarly edition of *Modern Chivalry*—argue that, within the entirety of the work, which was published in installments over several decades, there is a gradual shift from one position to another (22–25).

The fact that these reasonable but competing readings of *Modern Chivalry* coexist is itself telling. One common explanation relates to the picaresque genre itself—that it is necessarily dialogic. Those who take this line often celebrate this dialogism as a projection of the idealized political dynamics of the early American republic: the dawn of an inclusive if contentious democracy. The critic Cathy Davidson writes:

> By its very structure—or more accurately its structurelessness—the picaresque allowed the early American novelist numerous fictive possibilities. . . . The picaresque constructs its own politics or polis, a crazy quilt of American attitudes and practices. The loosest subgenre of all, it hovers ever on the edge of a formalistic collapse under the burden of its own inclusiveness. . . . The end product of this rhetorical and narrative seesaw is not some fictional utopia—the ideal America—but a raw (if energetic) Republic, a diverse and divided society in which the inherent contradictions of Republican discourse have not been totalized. (248–49)

This line of reasoning holds that the lack of a clear, single political position means that there is no single dominating voice, either Federalist or Jeffersonian. What emerges instead is a celebration of the value of contentiousness, of messy dialogue. The peripatetic squabbling, remarkable for its slippery incompleteness and its comic inability to be still, embodies an energetic national dialogue that resists any single, all-encompassing voice; it speaks to a state that sees itself as collectively authored. As intellectual historian Jay Fliegelman states, in writing about the "Unrealizable Ideal of Democratic Conversation" in the early Republic, "Productive horizontal conversation is never the easy back-and-forth colloquy fantasized as a foundational article of early democratic faith. In reality it is rough and tumble obliqueness coursing through triangulation, textualization, withholding, flattery, indifference, conversion, placation, entrapment, performance, displacement, and one-sided harangues" (101).

Dialogism and disputation: this was key to the construction of democratic national selfhood in both North and Latin America. And it had a parallel in another challenging unruliness: the vastness of nature. Nature was a looming presence that needed to be harmonized with man, or at least brought into an equal exchange.[5] Literary critic Christopher Looby points to emblematic cases where the scientific taxonomy of the natural world was paired with the self-fashioning impulse of the new nation. Citing some important observers of the early republic, Looby notes that "the obsession with natural harmony that marks the period in America would seem to mask an anxiety about the political dissonance that also marks the period" ("Taxonomy" 269). For instance, Looby writes, in Thomas Jefferson's *Notes on the State of Virginia* (1785), "the dynamics of social change often aroused in Jefferson a reactionary anxiety," and the descriptions of the land, the climate, flora, and fauna convey the belief that "the only kind of society that had any chance to forestall the process of corruption was one that was conflict free: [a] homogeneous, egalitarian, agricultural republic" (264–65). This impulse is also evident in what is considered to be the first museum in North America: Charles Willson Peale's Philadelphia Museum, opened in the 1780s, which organized nature along comprehensible, and calming, Linnaean taxonomic categories.

The debate about the symbolic importance of the nature of the Americas (including Spanish America) has a long history, as Antonello Gerbi has explored in *The Dispute of the New World* (1973). Beginning with the first encounter by European explorers, this wide-ranging argument evolved with the times and gathered strength in the eighteenth century, when it was framed in new scientific paradigms and methodologies. From the moment Europeans gained awareness that there was an entire, previously unknown continent that was not Europe, the aim of many natural philosophers and scientists was to prove that America's geography, flora, and fauna—and, by extension, its native and nativized cultures—were "small" in comparison with those of Europe. America was a stunted double, or stuck in at an earlier point of development. Natural philosophers including Cornelius de Pauw, George-Louis Leclerc (Comte de Buffon), William Robertson, and Guillaume Raynal made this claim, which was politically and intellectually expedient for a number of European constituencies and agendas from many parts of the political spectrum. It was cited by the French *Encyclopedistes,* it can be heard in German *Naturphilosophie,* and it echoes in the work of countless artists, poets, and musicians.

There was a pushback, naturally. Within Europe itself there were dedicated defenders of the Americas who argued on the opposing side. The discourse enraged North America's own Thomas Jefferson to the point that he asked the governor of New Hampshire to order soldiers to hunt down a gigantic moose so it could be sent to Buffon in France. Another notable defender of the Americas was the Prussian polymath and naturalist Alexander von Humboldt (1769–1859), one of the period's most important scientist-traveler.

This debate relates to another modern concept being (re)postulated during this period: the notion of American exceptionalism. One way of looking at exceptionalism is to consider it as a reply to this anti-American discourse instead of as a religious or intellectual mandate descended from Puritan notions about the "city on the hill": a self-affirming reaction to those arguments about Europe's natural superiority. Seen this way, exceptionalism becomes a reasonable defense against claims about American inferiority. And North American exceptionalism would thus share origins with the Latin American variant, which also developed quite prominently during the nineteenth century in the *americanista* discourse of Andrés Bello, José María Heredia, Domingo Faustino Sarmiento, and José Martí. These intellectuals and national foundational figures were deeply committed both to describing the uniqueness of the natural world of the Americas and to building a sense of national identity through it.

Art historian Barbara Stafford's important work on the nature art of the eighteenth century describes how scientific techniques and technological advances inflected the aesthetics of the period. The imagery in academic landscape painting of the time—Arcadian, heroic, and rustic—became progressively influenced by the growing technical precision coming from scientific sources. Scientific description itself was being transformed by new instrumentation, techniques, and classificatory rigor. For instance, cartography had developed considerably through advances in chronographs, and topographical illustration was more and more precise because of new optical instruments, printing technology, and even aerial perspectives made possible by ballooning. Technology led to what Stafford calls the "scientific gaze," entailing "a purposive curiosity that goes hand in hand with the utilitarian ideal of 'spreading knowledge'" (40).

This found a ready home in the large-format illustrated travel accounts that became fashionable during the latter half of the century. Humboldt's hugely popular and influential illustrated travel accounts included *Vues des Cordillères, et monumens des peuples indigenes de l'Amérique* (1816–24), economic and cultural descriptions such as his *Political Essays* about Mexico (1811) and Cuba (1825–26), travel journals, and essay collections on methodology such as *Views of Nature* (1808), one of Charles Darwin's favorite books.

Humboldt and fellow traveler botanist Aimé Bonpland walked on and described many of the same American roads that both Concolorcorvo and Brackenridge did. Although literary scholar Mary Louise Pratt claims that Humboldt's descriptions of the Americas deploy what she calls a colonizing "imperial eye," other interpreters such as Ottmar Ette (and I) have argued the exact opposite: that Humboldt's cultural and natural descriptions offer the *vues* of a European traveler who encounters the limits of his powers of vision and description, consequently developing a sense of cultural relativity (Ochoa 84–85). When Humboldt reaches the vast backcountry of the Americas—the "ends of civilization"—he also acknowledges the limits of his own acquisitive gaze, and he gains an awareness of the native Other as a separate and even inscrutable agency. He bumps into what the Peruvian Marxist critic Antonio Cornejo Polar calls the "pressure of the referent" (Paoli and Cornejo 259).[6]

At the very least, Humboldt wanted to correct the prejudiced distortions of natural philosophers like Buffon and Raynal, whose anti-American agenda was both programmatic and unfair. Humboldt's entry into the "Dispute of the New World" is an optimistic vision of the continent at a new dawn. His representation of the Americas—particularly weighty because it came from such an important voice (he was one of the last celebrated scientists to try to "know everything")—was heard in high places across Europe.

But, most important, his voice was heard within America itself. For instance, the description of what he saw in Mexico and Cuba in the *Political Essays* contains a thinly veiled critique of Spanish colonialism. The Spanish crown is subtly indicted for evils such as economic stagnation, poor land management, inflexible social distinctions, and—quite remarkably for the period—slavery. The effect of Humboldt's and Bonpland's trips on American founding independentists such as Simón Bolívar, who was looking for validation of his cause, is widely accepted. Mexican historian Enrique Krauze sums up the view about Humboldt's place in Latin American identity: "Humboldt was a midwife of [Latin American] consciousness. . . . Essentially, he gave [it] naturalization papers into Western history" (22, my translation). Although critics such as Mary Louise Pratt hold that Humboldt's supposed authority to grant such "naturalization papers" makes him an agent of colonialism, his authority was unquestionably influential to a Spanish America trying to view itself as separate from Spain.[7]

When Humboldt conveyed an American landscape in positive and optimistic terms, it directly advanced the cause of the incipient American nations. When foundational nation-builders such as Bolivar and Andrés Bello determined to revisualize their nations and their people, they found a fellow traveler in the German explorer. The Prussian nobleman's opinion of the continent's potential—its culture as well as its natural and economic resources—impacted their concepts of a constitutional and representative government, antislavery, and the economic potential of independent American nations based on the richness of their nature. And Humboldt was offering apparently politically neutral scientific descriptions of the American landscape and society. Humboldt's subtle but direct strategy inspired many of the founding fathers to inscribe his values into their own projects of description as nation-building: we hear Humboldt's views of nature in Bello's signature nature poem "Agriculture in the Torrid Zone," in the Argentinian intellectual (and president) Domingo Sarmiento's *Facundo*, in the writing of the conservative Mexican historian Lucas Alamán, and of course in Bolívar. The mark of Humboldt's morning constitutional walk "here and there" through the Americas is almost everywhere; it is even in Gabriel García Márquez's novel *One Hundred Years of Solitude*. When the wise and ancient necromancer Melquíades, who had witnessed the beginning of time, lies dying, "the only thing that could be isolated in the rocky paragraphs was the insistent hammering on the word *equinox, equinox, equinox,* and the name of Alexander von Humboldt" (40).

Humboldt was there at the dawn. He still displayed the pragmatic optimism of the *Naturphilosophie* of the German philosophers Johann Gottlieb Fichte and Friedrich Wilhelm Joseph von Schelling that he had absorbed during his university years at Jena studying geology and mine administration. But he approached the coming Romantic revolution, which would reclaim subjectivity, by incorporating subjectivity into the process of scientific investigation itself—in an arguably scientific way. He came to acknowledge that the witnessing self is an integral part of the "impartial," methodical appreciation of nature, allowing it as much space as any of the natural wonders under observation.

In good Romantic fashion, Humboldt conflated his descriptions of nature's grandiosity with the individual's act of perception—a fitting maneuver, given his position on the verge of a rational Enlightenment scientism that was quickly yielding to the new sensibility. This compromise was very much like that of his scientist-poet friend Goethe. Enlightened and objective observer Humboldt reveals Humboldt the somewhat humble personal storyteller, whose own awareness—his "fugitive ideas"—flutters about like intriguing butterflies, but in all fairness must be recorded as yet another element of nature, like a barometric reading, botanical sample, or mountain elevation (*Personal* xix).

Like Goethe's scientific studies on plant leaves and the optical essence of colors, which imply that the phenomena he describes are first of all products of perception that exist because of the eye of the beholder, Humboldt moves to encode the subject onto the object (Goethe 72). Humboldt still hopes for the Enlightenment ideal of making observation "safe from all passion," but he makes space for what I have elsewhere called a "naturalized self"—a subjective response to the surrounding world that is very much *part* of that physical world he is describing (87).

At the Edge of the "Natural"

Casta paintings are a well-known eighteenth-century genre of Spanish American portraiture. This genre was practiced widely in the colonial Hispanic world, with the most notable examples coming from the viceroyalties of Mexico and Peru. Usually created by academically trained artists, they exemplify Barbara Stafford's technological "scientific eye": human subjects observed like fauna in its natural habitat. This represented an attempt to classify racial categories using the rationalist scientific ethos of the period. The unruliness of miscegenation is normalized into a set of hierarchically arranged portraits, each composed similarly to convey a kind of parity.

The paintings show academic knowledge of botany, zoology, and geography, as well as the influence of technical drafting. The racial classifications they codify are meant to appear as impartial and dispassionate as any scientific illustrations of birds or mollusks. These works hide the true disciplinary intention—to uphold social hierarchy—behind a spectacle of masterful technical and scientific neutrality. And, like the quixotic/picaresque, the paintings insist on their own unvarnished, eyewitnessed truth, despite the social reality into which they crash.

A casta series typically catalogs all the possible combinations of Indian, European, and African blood in a particular corner of the Spanish Empire. Individual paintings in a series generally present a group of three people: both parents and their resulting mixed-race child. There is generally a text giving basic information, usually the popular term for the racial mixture represented: "From Spaniard and *meztiza*, quarteroon"; "From Quinteroon of Mulatto and Spaniard, *requinterona*"; "From cambujo and Indian, stand-in-the-air"; and so on. A given series presents a complete report of social standings and would be displayed in a public place such as a church or an administrative building.

These paintings are both aesthetic and disciplinary objects. While beautifully executed and extremely detailed, they are meant to keep everyone in check, as in two examples (see figs. 1 and 2) from a 1763 series by the Mexican academician Miguel Cabrera (1695–1768).

The social context—the "habitats" of these racial mixes (in these cases, a commercial setting and perhaps a kitchen)—is shown with an almost

Figure 1. *De español y de India, nace mestiza* (*From Spaniard and Indian, a Mestiza Is Born*), Miguel Cabrera, 1763. Oil on canvas. (Private collection, Mexico)

Figure 2. *De Español y Albina, Torna Atrás* (*From Spaniard and Albino, Backwards-Jumper*), Miguel Cabrera, 1763. Oil on canvas. (Private collection, Mexico)

nonchalant air of impartiality. External concerns (e.g., commerce, ownership, selfhood, class disparity) are present but muted. The subject is clearly the couple and their child, not the context, the consequences of their generative act, or the transgression of miscegenation. But scientific modesty does not quite erase the transgressions. In another example (see fig. 3, ca. 1725) from a series attributed to José de Ibarra (1685–1756), there is the strong possibility that the union between a well-dressed "Spaniard" and an "Indian" woman, which has produced the "mestizo" child, is extramarital. This is visible in the somewhat atypical presence of two children instead of the usual one.

Which of the two is the mixed-race mestizo product of this union: the blond baby, or the servant boy carrying it? Could it be that *both* are this man's offspring? Are both the woman and her older child in fact the servants of this Spaniard, living in some off-site *casa chica* (little house), while the white baby is the legitimate offspring of the man's *casa grande* (big house)? Both products are his, one legitimate and the other not. The strong suggestion of this unequal arrangement pretends to rise above social judgment via the painter's almost gentle and equalizing scientific

48 *Fellow Travelers*

Figure 3. *De español e india, mestizo* (*From Spainard and Indian, Mestizo*), José de Ibarra, 1725, oil on canvas, 164 × 91 cm. (Museo de América, Madrid)

gaze. It is simply, painstakingly, accurate. The lushness of the displayed items of commerce in the background suggest that no one is too badly off; there is some measure of security for everybody. The inscribed injustice is muted to the point of comfort by the aesthetics.

The fiction in the flattening visual language of the casta paintings presents all mother-father-child triads uniformly, however unequal and charged with undertones of inequality or violence they may be. The subjects are somehow on equal footing as *subjects;* the artists' tools of observation and classification regulate and equalize the categorical reality. The illegitimacy is legitimate as a *subject,* and as worthy of observation and description as any significant flora or fauna, natural habitat, or topographical feature of the land. These paintings provide a regulating and categorizing mechanism, much like the superimposed grid lines of the surveyors who ventured into the new backcountry.

It is a kind of blindness. It is, essentially, stupidity.

However, this flattening and normative blindness had a countervoice. Like many cultured art forms, the *cuadros de castas* generated folk imitations by local artists and artisans who were not academically trained. A look at some of these popular interpretations reveals the supposed impartiality of the genre they imitated. This is because "untrained" popular artists did not always know enough to conform to the conventions and thematic limits of their more academic formal models; their "naturalized" and often quite fanciful versions of the genre break the discreet limits of what should be shown. Figure 4 shows an example from one such folk series from the late eighteenth century.

Figure 4. *De español y negra, mulata* (*From Spaniard and Black comes Mulatta*), unknown artist, ca. 1775–1800. Oil on canvas, 36 x 48 cm. (Museo de América, Madrid)

The neutrality of the academic artist's "scientific eye" is punctured by this frank depiction: the serene uniformity and impartiality so carefully curated in Cabrera's series is here set aside, or, more likely, simply ignored. An honest and unsettling reality breaks right through—in this case, domestic violence, something that would have been glossed over by the genteel Cabrera. A gruesome truth is allowed in by the artist-observer, who is simply not aware that he's not supposed to show this.[8]

This coexistence of blindness with clueless insight is comparable to the detailed information that coexists with the stories of the stupid traveling pairs of *El Lazarillo* and *Modern Chivalry*. In both Concolorcorvo and Brackenridge, blinding stupidity is offset in good measure by contradicting transparency and literal bluntness. When the reality of the world breaks in, it is truthful precisely because of the contrast with the travelers' inability to see what is in front of them for what it is.

What happens to the Other under this scheme of observation, to Cornejo Polar's "pressure of the referent"? Considering the descriptive practices of ethnography, cultural historian James Clifford asks an interesting question about the distinction between the subject and the object of field study. In twentieth-century ethnographic field observation, the Other is very much a part of the observation process. This is because the ethnographer is a participant-observer and inserts him- or herself into otherness, actively interacting and even collaborating with the objects of study and the resulting story—to the point that Clifford asks, "Who is *actually* the author of the field notes?" (45).

In partial answer to this question, Clifford offers the case of the surrealist artist-turned-ethnographer Marcel Griaule, who ventured to West Africa in the early 1930s to observe the Dogon people. Griaule approached his task quite bombastically, inserting himself as meddlesomely as possible. He dug up sacred sites at midnight, kept a stable of paid "informants" sure to tell him what he wanted to hear, and terrorized locals with an airplane. His activities were so annoying to the community under observation/siege that it had to react *somehow*. Griaule had absolutely no pretense of maintaining discreet distance or neutrality, not to mention basic courtesy, in his interactions with his subjects. Rather, he deliberately planted himself as an irritant, just to see how the culture would react. His aim was more specific than the usual ethnographic role of simply and carefully sketching a panorama of a given culture: he sought insight into how the culture managed interlopers, how it dealt with nasty outsiders (Clifford 56–91). The way Griaule approached Cornejo Polar's "pressure of the referent" was by putting unpleasant pressure back *on* that referent, on the Other. It was a kind of laboratory microcolonialism, created to see how the referent pressed back to irritation. He did away with the fiction of impartial engagement.

These, then, are the observers of the early American lands and people we have been considering: Alexander von Humboldt, with his tacit sincerity, who acknowledges his own subjectivity within scientific observation; the folk-artist reinterpreters of the cuadros de castas, who sidestep the safeguards of "neutral" observation; and the dunderheaded traveling pairs in *Modern Chivalry* and *A Guide for Blind Travelers*. In all three of these cases, the observers surreptitiously insert themselves into their studies, as modern ethnographers would do. In doing so, they reveal the pressure of the referent as the observed subjects push back. And, in each case, their insights are often the result of what they *fail* to see or acknowledge.

In the case of the quixotic duos, the engagement with their object (what's out there) is quite lopsided. At first blush this pair of pairs seems to epitomize what philosopher Avital Ronell defines as stupidity. Despite the repeated startling encounters with the world through which they travel—something that would lead most (normal) human beings into self-awareness, knocking some sense into them—these characters remain insistently and stubbornly stupid. The pairs appear unable to see *themselves* in that world, and "no mirror yet has been invented in which they might reflect themselves. They ineluctably evade reflection. No catoptrics can mirror back to them, these shallowest, most surface-bound beings," as Ronell says of the stupid (18). Yet I would argue that, in this particular case, that mirror *has* been invented: it is the road. Or, rather, a mirror has been built around them, because others are allowed see what these travelers are missing—and this is possible precisely *because* of the blindness that keeps them moving through the "here and there."

The catalog of places, institutions, people, habits, and injustices that scrolls by in both *Modern Chivalry* and *A Guide for Blind Travelers* is penetrating and insightful, and even useful. This doesn't mean that the protagonists aren't genuinely stupid or blind. They remain so busy engaging each other that they continue not seeing the world around them for what it is, even though they are very much within it. They seem immune to the famously mind-broadening effect of travel: they see only imperfectly what would be seen by more perceptive travelers, like the lonely traveler/survivor. When the lonely and hungry "true" picaro walks into a situation, he "gets it"; he might forced to comply and adapt, or to move on. But the pair of stupid and optimistic travelers who set out in the early morning to mark the world often fail to capture it for themselves, leaving it instead for the reader to witness as they stumble into one mess after another.

Allowed Fools

Why send out such a stupid pair of rogues—blind ones, to boot—to survey, see what's out there, and have such an active part in documenting the new land? Because, in truth, these delinquents are not as challenging to the order of things as their roguehood might lead one to think. The order of things sanctions their surveying mission and expects them to conform in certain ways when they report back. They stumble into many ludicrous and unsettling situations, revealing undersides of the land and peoples through which they travel: they fall off cliffs when they go out to pee and get into numerous fistfights, and they engage in misunderstandings about things important to the locals. Their ignorant intrusions often challenge established habits and customs, all to great comic effect. The cliffs, pitfalls, and habits remain in place and unchanged by these visitors, but they still call for reporting. The pair doesn't alter or undermine in any fundamental way what they see in the land; their traveling show stays in its own separate world, and the two worlds do not necessarily engage or affect each other.

In a parenthetical critique of philosopher Mikhail Bakhtin's concept of the yearly carnival celebration, British literary theorist Terry Eagleton quietly notes a disquieting truth about its (allegedly) subversive nature: "Carnival, after all, is a *licensed affair* in every sense, a permissible rupture of hegemony, a contained popular blow-off as disturbing and relatively ineffectual as a revolutionary work of art. As Shakespeare's Olivia remarks, there is no slander in an allowed fool" (148). Bakhtin casts the carnivalesque as liminal and revolutionary—normal laws and conventions are suspended in order to celebrate this rite of passage. But as Eagleton notes, it is actually *conservative* in a literal sense. The topsy-turvy chaos of carnival comes every year, with a precise predictability, to the point that it actually reinforces the preexisting patterns of society: this is self-affirming parody, a sanctioned and temporary suspension of the law. After the blowout, the status quo is restored. In fact, the period of anarchy has reinforced it; there was never really a risk of true collapse.[9]

In another apparent upheaval of the status quo, during the late eighteenth century the Spanish Empire was engaged in a calculated reinvention, attempting to shore itself up after more than a century of steady decline. Before the Napoleonic invasion and the wars of independence of the early nineteenth century hit it hard, the Bourbon government of Charles III implemented an ambitious administrative makeover. Spurred by fear of another revolution like the one in France Revolution, the crown was keen to revitalize its profile and its economy and to maintain the increasingly tenuous income stream from its New World possessions. The crown realized that it had to rethink centuries of bureaucratic inefficiency and the role of ingrained institutions such as the church and hereditary business monopolies. Some historians even refer to this time as an "internal revolution," a national makeover that extended to the colonies.

One of the main problems was a system of parallel legal systems, each with its own rights, courts, and legal protections. These systems, the *fueros,* were held by the church and the military; accountable only to themselves, they essentially diluted the authority of the crown. These self-sustaining systems had worked adequately in economically flusher times, but that was no longer the case. The central government began a process to break inherited land and property monopolies, a development known colorfully as the *desamortización de las manos muertas,* or "impounding from dead hands."

The stranglehold on important institutions had ensured that trade in and out of Spain's overseas colonies occurred only under legacy-held controls, and commerce with countries outside of Spain was strictly regulated. All shipping to and from Spain had to be conducted through select ports closely held by a few entities, sometimes even single families with royal licenses, or *cédulas.* All American goods had to travel—inefficiently and expensively—first to Spain, where they accrued tariffs, before they could be exported to the rest of the world, even right back to the Americas as manufactured products. Direct trade with other American or European countries was illegal, even with other Spanish American ports or with British or French colonies that were much nearer to the ports of origin.

The Decree of Free Trade of 1778 represented a concerted effort to break up the monopolies, open trade, and spread the wealth. This trust-busting came at the expense of the small ruling class that been in power for centuries, siphoning off the slowly decreasing profit margins. The decree allowed the growing and hungry middle class into the mix: the American-born white merchants and entrepreneurs, *criollos,* or "Creole Pioneers," as Benedict Anderson calls them (47–65). These criollos had for centuries held second-class citizenship in their own land, always deferring to the recently arrived Spaniards (*indianos*) that were regularly shipped in from Europe to fill most of the top positions.

As part of its administrative reinvention, the crown saw an opportunity to increase competition and defuse the long-simmering resentment of criollos against the constantly arriving Spaniards, who occupied the places they considered rightfully theirs. The damage to the monopolies would be worth it to the Crown. As historian David Brading puts it, "The effects of these ... reforms upon the great merchant houses of Mexico City was remarkable. They found the age of relatively safe monopoly profits had ended. They were confronted with a more vigorous and numerous competition" (*Bourbon* 115).

Another key element of administrative reinvention was an optimistic investment in the local infrastructures needed to open the new trade routes: roads, ports, and communications systems. New types of functionaries and bureaucrats—"inspectors" like the visitador Alonso Carrió de la Vandera—were the agents and implementers of such change. As historian Ruth Hill says, although the motive for Concolorcorvo's book is clearly "Menippean satire," travel "was a *material* motive for Carrió: he was commissioned to inspect and reform the posts and to write up a report" (18).

Here is the "however." As previously mentioned, the established opinion among leading historians such as David Brading and Anthony Pagden is that the Bourbon reforms afforded the colonial criollo class a new sense of possibility and offered a new dawn. They opened a door to a class that had long felt stifled by colonial overrule, ultimately creating the suggestion of actual independence. As criollos developed economic self-sufficiency, according to this widely held view, this set in place an expectation of political and cultural independence—despite the Crown's initial intention to staunch such unrest through controlled liberalization.[10] The match was lit when Napoleon invaded Spain and replaced the weak if legitimate king, sparking Latin American independence movements. Some of these insurrections were led, paradoxically enough, by criollos claiming they were the more loyal Spaniards: they were more Spanish than the king, if that king was Joseph Bonaparte. This echoes the paradox at the beginning of the independent United States. The Boston insurrections began with a demand to become *more* legitimately English, not less—for colonials to have the same rights as any other British subject, including equal representation in Parliament, if they were to be taxed as British subjects.

Recently, though, economic historians have nuanced this established reading of the (supposed) opportunities given to the criollo class during the late colonial period. It is true that loosened trade controls led to the legitimation of an increasingly independent criollo merchant class, mostly in the provincial cities, granted license (at the expense of monopolistic concerns) to export local materials and trade European manufactured goods on their own. Some of these new merchants were even given tacit permission to engage in contraband trade with the British and French colonies of the Caribbean.[11] But, as economic historian John Fisher and others have emphasized, overall control of trade was still held by the Crown and its approved agents. In the "liberalizing" reforms of 1778, the powers that be remained intact.

Fisher contends that the decree of 1778 produced no real power shift, no real revolution, other than a rearrangement of which white European-blood group shared its profits with the Crown. "The commercial 'freedom' defined by the 1778 *reglamento*," laments Fisher, "was a strictly limited one" ("Imperial" 22). This limited freedom was part of the larger design by the metropolis of the Bourbon Empire to reenergize *trade itself,* via a calculated release of pressure: an "allowed" reform, just short of actual revolution. It was not meant to effect a fundamental shift in power. The trade routes themselves, and the structures and energies that maintained them, remained essentially unchallenged. The "Decree of Free Trade" was a foreshadowing of the twentieth-century North American Free Trade Agreement (NAFTA) that "opened" markets while actually imposing neoliberal constraints and internal tariffs. This is Eagleton's "licensed affair" of "allowed fools" who dare to "critique" empire.[12]

Our quixotic duos are the allowed fools of empire: Don Alonso and Calixto on the one hand, Captain Farrago and Teague on the other. And "exploring the margins of society," as the critic Cathy Davidson affirms, they belong to the same class as the visual artists of the castas, as the museum cataloguers, and as the future-president grid surveyors who set out to organize what is out there for the purpose of nation-building (249). Although these half-blind traveling pairs are creatures of the margins, their goal is crucial the new nations aspiring to find and establish their own centrality, and on the verge of rearranging their own world.

As travelers they are beholden to—and report to—future forms with new centers of power, no longer Europe. Those new centers cannot but echo their immediate predecessors, the previous form of empire. The "narrator" of *A Guide for Blind Travelers* is a rogue member of the *hampa*—not to mention being an Indian, that most marginalized of racial underclasses—and he supposedly directs his intelligence report to fellow members of this underclass. But this is brownface: postcolonial mimicry in reverse. The actual witness, and actual writer, is Don Alonso Carrió de la Vandera, visitador or post road inspector, Spanish born, and an unmistakable instrument of empire. His express commission from the Crown of His Royal Highness King Charles was to see what was out there, and to take accurate notes and file a credible report. For the most part, he succeeded.

Except for the stupid part.

2 Dying Pastoral

The Power of Homology and Other Disappearances into the Open Ranges of *Martín Fierro* and *The Searchers* (and "Brokeback Mountain")

> Every valley shall be exalted, and every mountain and hill shall be made low:
> and the crooked shall be made straight, and the rough places plain.
> —Isaiah 40:4

IN HIS poem "Texas," Jorge Luis Borges ponders the similarity between the Argentine Pampas and the Old West:

> Here, too. Here as at the other edge
> Of the hemisphere, an endless plain
> Where a man's cry dies a lonely death.
> Here too the Indian, the lasso, the wild horse.
>   (207, translated by Mark Strand)

These two similar biomes led to a cultural version of what ecologists call "convergent evolution," in which comparable conditions cause unrelated species to develop the same physical adaptations. These grassland regions of the Americas became the habitats of free-range, seminomadic horseback herders. Open-range culture is not unique to the US Southwest and Argentina, of course. In the Northern Hemisphere it has occurred worldwide, roughly along the 40th parallel, wherever we find expansive grasslands: Extremadura in Spain, southeastern Kazakhstan on the Asian steppes, the state of Kansas. In the Southern Hemisphere a similar climatic line runs somewhat closer to the equator, around the 30th parallel. The largest ranch in the world, Anna Creek Station, has been in operation at latitude 28.9 in Australia's Northern Territories since the 1860s. The "Center Region" of Argentina (Córdoba, Santa Fe, Entre Ríos) runs right along the 30th parallel.

Not surprisingly, the skills, technologies, and cultures that developed in these places are similar. But the similarities between the two cultures that developed in the Americas during the mid-nineteenth century are particularly striking—perhaps because they shared common Spanish origins, and the changes took place during the same period of industrial technological advancement. A few examples include single-handed reining; lassoing techniques to bring down wayward cattle relatively unharmed; and the wearing of soft, broad-brimmed hats and leather leg protectors. Both open-range drivers and gauchos dealt with feral horses that required "breaking": training them to respond to delicate foot and even toe commands. Valuable abilities included tracking animals and people over long distances and divining for water in a parched landscape. Utiliarian tools such as pistols, blades, and whips, when used as offensive weapons, led to forms of stylized dueling.

Shared cultural and social patterns emerged as well. Like medieval bards, balladeers sang newsy epics and engaged in public competitions in front of mostly illiterate audiences. The horse-bound men who followed the herds often abandoned their subsistence homesteads for extended periods, leaving women and children to fend for themselves until (and if) they returned. Rudimentary honor codes of justice and retribution quickly turned men into outlaws—and, when that happened, it was easy for them to disappear into the vast, unpopulated land. Eventually, technological advances such as the railroad, the telegraph, barbed wire, and repeating firearms affected and ultimately ended this culture. Both the Pampas and the US West contained significant indigenous populations that had also adopted the horse. In both regions government-sponsored projects of genocide were directed against those native peoples, especially when they resisted colonization of their lands and forced relocation to far less favorable territories.

For our purposes, another important parallel between North and South are the fierce bonds of loyalty that developed between the men who worked together on the open range. The Argentinean epic poem *The Gaucho Martín Fierro* by José Hernández tells of such a bond between two gauchos. This poem belongs to a highly unusual genre, the "gauchesque." Generally imitations of the epics sung by gaucho balladeers or *payadores,* these gauchesque works were cultivated mimicry, mostly written by provincial intellectuals assuming the voice of a gaucho. Few actual gaucho songs have been preserved, but linguists, ethnomusicologists, and historians agree that this invented literary genre quite accurately captures the words and ethos of the gauchos.

The intentions behind these imitations were mixed. Some were classist parodies—extended redneck jokes, making fun of the hayseeds. For instance, in Estanislao del Campo's "Fausto" (1866), a gaucho stumbles into a provincial opera house and watches in amazement a performance of Gounod's *Faust;* the poem is a humorous, wide-eyed report of what he saw. Other gauchesque works were sincere attempts to represent a way of life. Notable examples include Bartolomé Hidalgo's "Patriotic Dialogues" (1822); Hilario Ascasubi's "Aniceto the Rooster" (1853) and "Santos Vega and the Twins of la Flor" (1851); and Antonio Lussich's "Three Eastern Gauchos" (1872). As with US cowboy culture, some gauchesque works took on actual historical figures—for instance, the life of the outlaw Juan Moreiras (1829–1874) earned many retellings, and the regional gaucho strongman Juan Facundo Quiroga (1788–1835) was described in Domingo Sarmiento's influential and deeply complicated portrait *Facundo* (1845). But most gauchesque works featured fictional protagonists.[1]

This wave of ventriloquized gauchos captured the imagination of the educated reading public of Argentina, and well beyond. The genre's sheer creativity and colorful local flavor secured it a place at the center of Latin American literary history—much like the Western genre that eventually gained a central place in US culture. Arguably, the crowning text in this corpus is Hernández's *Martín Fierro,* published in two parts—the "Departure" in 1872 and the "Return" in 1879. Its length, complex structure, and intricate moral concerns reveal a cultivated lineage owing much to the epic tradition stretching back to the Epic of Gilgamesh, but the voice and the action are deeply local. Its frame narrative has a *payador* taking to a public stage and—in a typical gauchesque gesture—issuing a challenge for someone to beat him in a singing face-off.

The narrator, Fierro, then tells his own life story, since he is both a singer and a range outlaw—not an uncommon pairing. He spins a familiar tale of a subsistence gaucho whose punishment on a trumped-up charge (in his case, not voting in the local rigged elections) is conscription into the regional military force. Fierro relates how he spent most of this time in the private workforce for the local *caudillo,* or strongman: "The Colonel would send us out/to work in his own fields" (25). Whenever actually sent on military missions to fight Indians, his troops are given comically inadequate weapons and no ammunition, because that had long ago been sold to ostrich hunters. Still, in hand-to-hand combat on one such outing, Fierro manages to kill an Indian, the son of a chief. He does this with nothing but the true gaucho tools of *bolas* (a kind of boomerang/lasso) and knife. Fierro sings that, after serving obediently as a conscript for a lengthy time, he ultimately had little to show for his efforts—no salary or even any idea of when his service would end. When he complains, he is punished. He decides on the usual path in stories of gaucho conscription: he deserts.

The story of the gaucho deserter is historically significant. Conscription—the *leva*—was a long-standing method of controlling the rural peasantry and extracting free labor. For generations the wily gaucho had been a useful tool for many projects of domestication and settlement. The latest way of forcing conscription was to require documentation—land deeds, birth certificates, marriage licenses. This instantly turned members of this mostly illiterate class into squatters, "vagrants," and criminals. In the subsequent gaucho mythology that emerged, the deserting gaucho was often cast as a free spirit who had been unjustly persecuted. This reinforced the romantic myth of his anti-institutional individualism, a figure out of step with modernity and at odds with the national project of "civilizing" the frontier: a primeval and atavistic figure more in tune with the land than with the whims of the metropolis. One powerful and common reading of *Martín Fierro* is as an extended protest against modernity and the encroaching tentacles of empire.[2]

When the deserter Martín Fierro finally makes his way home, he finds his homestead empty. He learns from neighbors that his small herd has been sold, his young sons have been farmed out ("How could anybody expect them to work? They were still like young pigeons that hadn't feathered out!"), and his woman has taken up with "some ladies' man, I guess to get the bread I wasn't around to give her" (46–47). Seeking a drink at a local *pulpería*—a saloon/trading post common throughout South America—he makes overtures toward a mulatto woman and is challenged by her man. What happens next echoes the description in *El Lazarillo: A Guide for Blind Travelers* (1773) of the coarse goings-on of hungry gauchos who gathered and wanted something to eat:

> Frequently . . . these men get together under pretext of going to the country to amuse themselves, taking no provisions for their sustenance other than a lasso, *bolas,* and a knife. One day they will agree to eat the rump of a cow or a calf; they lasso it, throw it down, and with its four feet securely tied, they pull from it, almost alive, the entire rear quarter with its hide, and making a few punctures in the side of the meat, they roast it badly and devour it half raw without any condiment except a little salt, if by chance they are carrying some. Other times they kill a cow or a calf merely to eat the *matambre,* the meat between the ribs and the skin (55).

The gauchos kill nonchalantly for a single cut of meat. Fierro kills his man just as casually. Highlighting just how perfunctory his violence is, he sings:

> Finally we tangled, and
> I lifted him with my knife
> And, like a bag of bones,
> Tossed him against a fence.
> He let out a few kicks
> And sang for the butcher.
> . . . .
> I wiped my blade on the grass,
> untied my frisky colt,
> got on slow and rode off
> toward the lowlands. (53–54)

There is a deadening similarity to the violent acts that happen in this place. One approximates the next so closely that they might all be the same act, whether it's a man or a steer being killed.

In the climactic moment of the "Departure," Fierro has killed once again and is being actively pursued by the law. Cornered by a military posse like the one from which he and so many others have deserted, he puts up an unusually ferocious fight. He kills several of his pursuers but is about to be overpowered when a crucial event happens. This moment at the high point of the battle is held as a foundational center of modern Argentine literature, and, by extension, the very national identity.[3] A gaucho from the arresting posse named Cruz—a conscript like Fierro himself, whose familiar story doesn't need much introduction—is so moved by Fierro's rage and passion that he stops and roars to his comrades:

> Cruz won't stand
> for this! I won't let you bastards
> kill a brave man like this! (67)

He instantly switches sides and begins fighting alongside the outlaw and against his fellow troopers.

Cruz and Fierro are now a pair of deserters. They eventually defeat the posse, and once the battle is done they stack up the dead. At the very end of the "Departure," the narrating bard signs off by saying that "followin' their course exactly/they entered the wildlands [desierto]" (90). The only logical conclusion to their sudden pairing is for them to disappear into the true wilderness, the untamed desierto (different from the evolving backcountry), where the rule of law is still absent and where Indians, animals, and men like them run with the wind.

A Change of Climate

> The great open American spaces eventually ran out.
> —Michael Hardt and Antonio Negri, *Empire*

The significant transformation that happens to Cruz and Fierro between the two parts of *Martín Fierro* also happens to the poem itself: the tone, the themes, and even the stated aims are very different in the "Return." Martín seems to be done with fighting; he is no longer resisting the civilizing rule of law. Much of the second part is devoted to the search for his lost children so that he can admonish them, urge them to stop being gauchos in the old sense—to settle down and stop wandering, and to obey. It is a moralistic homily. The Martín of the second part is not the violent Martín of the first part.

The stark contrast between the "Departure" and the "Return" reflects a very real and very specific change to the land during the 1870s and 1880s. The Pampas—like the US West in the later nineteenth century—had been evolving rapidly. But, at the beginning of the 1870s (and between the appearance of the poem's two parts), the aggressive, state-sponsored project of Indian "pacification" had reached its highest point. By the later part of the decade, it had achieved its goal for a fairly vast stretch of land around Buenos Aires. The rule of law had begun to take root—the Pampas had stopped being true wilderness, desierto, and had turned into semisettled backcountry.

The immediate political precedent leading to this was a relative end to the sectarian violence that had paralyzed Argentina's population centers since independence. For decades the country had been consumed by debilitating conflict between factions favoring a loose confederation of semiautonomous provinces, or "Federalistas," and the (mostly educated) middle classes who wanted a centralized republic patterned on European liberal, democratic models, or "Unitarios" (Shumway 119–23; Bethell 63). But the Argentinian Constitution of 1853 provided a fairly stable political détente, and its normalizing effect had mostly taken effect by 1860. Attention could now be directed outward into what the country possessed, and could exploit, in the totality of its territory.

The newly stabilized metropolis projected a sense of national mission onto the provincias: it looked to its frontier as a place to grow economically and culturally. The freshly secured central government began to court European immigration to help build and populate the nation. Massive numbers of Spaniards and eastern Europeans, especially from southern Italy, were courted. At one point the conscript Fierro complains about an Italian immigrant who is part of his troop:

> Who knows where he come from!
> Maybe he warn't even a Christian,
> Since the only thing he said
> Was that he was a *Papolitano*
> . . . .
> I don't know why the government
> sends to the frontier
> a bunch of gringos that don't even
> know how to come up to a horse. (40–41)[4]

The main problem in the vast grassland areas radiating from the River Plate basin, where the government began focusing its attention, was caused by periodic stampede/cattle raids known as *malones*. Similar to raids repelled in the southwestern United States and northern Mexico during this same period, these were carried out by the Mapuche, Ranquel, and Pampa Indians. Romanticized paintings from both regions portray feathered braves riding bareback on feral horses. The example in figure 5 depicts a Mapuche raid, but it could easily be portraying the Comanches or Apaches of western North America.

The massive genocidal campaign known as the "Taming of the Wilderness" (*conquista del desierto*) was complemented by crude but large-scale works—linked forts, towers, and a system of trenches (*zanjas de Alsina*)—extending for hundreds of miles to contain the Indians until they could be systematically exterminated. Gaucho conscription intensified. As a result of this concentrated effort, enormous stretches of land became open for white agriculture and settlement within a matter of a few years.[5]

This became a time to determine who and what would be allowed into the newly expanding nation. The peasant population of seminomadic rural whites and mestizos living in subsistence conditions—as exemplified by the gaucho—posed an existential dilemma to an expanding metropolis wooing modernity. This rural population had been tolerated up until now and even occasionally found useful. They had weathered the wars by

Figure 5. *El rapto (El Malón)* (*The abduction [The Indian raid]*), Johann Mortiz Rugendas, 1834. Oil on canvas, 43.2 × 50.8 cm. (Private collection, Santiago de Chile; photo © Christie's Images/Bridgeman Images)

staying out of the way and eking out a living in the still-untamed and unexploited lands, or by fighting on the side of whoever needed them the most. There'd been not much reason (or wherewithal) to curb the gaucho, his habitat, and his marginal lifestyle.

But the taming of the wilderness and the massive national consolidation that came with it changed the situation. The eradication of the Indians would be so complete that it would obviate the need for the gaucho as a tool of that project. The gauchos themselves now became the problem. Their small, isolated homesteads stood in the way of the large ranching and farming concerns beginning to reshape the land. The nature of available work was quite different from traditional open-range cattle driving. The colossal seasonal drives were over. This all sounds like the North American West, and the old saw that the railroad and barbed wire killed the cowboy. What Borges says about the Old West—"Here, too. Here as at the other edge/of the hemisphere"—also resonates in the Pampas (*Poems*

207). Much of the usable land was quickly fenced into semi-industrial cattle complexes. What had recently been open grazing lands now became large feedlots and raising pens. Railroads brought in farmed fodder and returned with live cattle to slaughterhouses in exploding population centers like Buenos Aires, Kansas City, and Chicago, as well as points east. Improved industrial tools, water management, and new weaponry accelerated the process.

In a scene in John Ford's classic Western film *The Searchers* (1956), a homesteading couple, the Jorgensens, argue about the death of their son at the hands of the Comanches. Old man Jorgensen questions why they are suffering so to carve out a place in such a hostile land:

JORGENSEN (*angrily*)
  It's this country killed my boy! . . . Yes, by golly!

MRS. JORGENSEN (*Mrs. Jorgensen stands.*)
  Now Lars! . . . It so happens we be Texicans. . . . We took a reachin' hold, way far out, past where any man has right or reason to hold on. . . . Or if we didn't, our folks did. . . . So we can't leave off without makin' them out to be fools, wastin' their lives 'n wasted in the way they died. . . . A Texican's nothin' but a human man out on a limb. . . . This year an' next and maybe for a hundred more. But I don't think it'll be forever. Someday this country will be a fine good place to be. . . . Maybe it needs our bones in the ground before that time can come.

(*The speech impresses everyone.*)

Mrs. Jorgensen is optimistically waiting for the inevitable change, the soon-to-come rule of law and the domestication it will bring. But first it means having some of the new arrivals die and be buried, "our bones in the ground," recalling the first settlers of Macondo in Gabriel Garcia Márquez's *One Hundred Years of Solitude:*

  "We will not leave," she said. "We will stay here, because we have had a son here."
  "We have still not had a death," he said. "A person does not belong to a place until there is someone dead under the ground." (13)

This coming domestication—the notion that the "country will be a fine good place to be"—is why the "Return" of *Martín Fierro* is so different from the "Departure." Fierro's values, which he now tries to instill in his sons, are dramatically changed from the earlier code of violence under which had lived in the "Departure." The outlaw pair of Fierro and

Cruz has almost inexplicably transformed during their time in the empty space of the wilderness. In the "Return," Fierro engages in a duel with yet another "Negro," who, it turns out, is the younger brother of the first man he had killed in the "Departure." But, instead of a knife fight, this time the duel is a singing face-off with the singer/gaucho Before, this would probably have ended in bloodshed, and, indeed, on several tense moments, it seems headed that way. But that doesn't happen. At the hottest point of the contest, recalling his first homicide, Martín taunts this younger man,

> A bunch of quarrelsome nigger boys
> In my times I guess I've met
> There were some top-notchers among them too,
> Quick of the eye and hand, I'm telling you. (288)

But this time he can control himself:

> Every man has got to pull
> In the yoke he's harnessed to;
> It's a long time since I picked a fight
> And in quarrelling I don't delight. (288, translated by Robert Owen)

Later in the poem, Fierro and Cruz gather their long-lost sons and learn about the lives of each of the young men. The "Return" concludes with an extended homily from Fierro, offering advice as an experienced "friend" rather than as a father, his guidance brimming with assimilationist values. He tells the sons that a man "must work to earn his bread" and "must not kill or fight for show; you have in my shame a mirror to see yourselves" (4655–56, my translation) When Martín stops his homily another balladeer picks up the story, explaining that now "the gaucho must have a home, school, church, and rights" (4826–27, my translation).

This is a departure from the "Departure," which had depicted Martín as a hardened gaucho who frigidly and perfunctorily knifes a man simply because he can—the display of cold-bloodedness is itself a valuable asset. In contrast, the "Return" brims with bourgeois values. When the storytelling comes to a close, Fierro and his sons make a momentous promise: they agree to abandon the family surname Fierro, or "iron" (301, translated by Owen). The hard metal is gone, left behind. This is an end to violence, and to the hard, blunt words associated with it. No longer will scores be settled the old way. Careful civil values—school and church, but also individual rights—will be the new lay of the land, the new "yoke he's harnessed to."

The End to the Loneliness

About the homologous "endless plains," Borges says that this is "where a man's cry dies a lonely death" (150). The myths of both the US range driver and the gaucho were built around the imminence of their demise. The conventional view that the indomitable Western spirit fell victim to a natural course of development was first formulated by Frederick Jackson Turner in his foundational essay "The Significance of the Frontier in American History" (1893), which begins with the 1890 census report announcing that the population of the West had reached critical density. Turner says with some regret that "this brief official statement marks the closing of a great historic movement" (1). The frontier, now closed to heroic acts of individual courage and ingenuity, was now ready to start generating a mythology—a mythology that began with an awareness of its own disappearance, an always-already posteriority lamenting a loss.

Here, Turner acknowledges that what had just been lost in the frontier was unrecoverable. While this was a nostalgic reading of the situation, it was not necessarily a negative one, announcing a decline. Rather, it marked a stylistic and tonal beginning, and Turner's thesis is essentially optimistic: it implies that future success and ingenuity was prefigured in America's pioneering spirit, and that it would continue with the permanent settlers to come later.

This overarching narrative casts the disappearance of the open range, and the horseman, as inevitable. The range rider's way of life could not have survived the natural course of progress. He was a primeval figure, and the modernization that rendered him obsolete also meant a triumph of civilization that he had in many ways invited. In both North and South America, the disappearing borderlands made the cowhand and the gaucho exemplary but transitional and primitive figures who would have needed to go at some point. A Texican, as Mrs. Jorgensen says, is "nothin' but a human man out on a limb"—at once a product of the unique American landscape and a repository of some spirit both ancient and constant, but now gone in its original form. The people who first ventured into the open range were a projection of a national self: good, brave, Edenic pioneers, pragmatic and resourceful, a "human man" whose qualities, when reduced to their elemental state in the crucible of the open prairie, reveal true grit.

But this masculine, true grit will inevitably clash with those same values when they have evolved under the sway of the metropolis. So a key part of the driver/gaucho story is its own demise in the face of the inevitable future: domestication by the metropolis (though it will not forget him and will even begin attributing its own success to him). Specifically in Latin America, gauchos have always been culturally associated with *criollismo,* a deep-roots identification with rural Spain—*España profunda.* Spain's place as the focal point of this working-class culture was now challenged by arrivals from Italy and central and eastern Europe, who held cultured France as its ideal rather than rural Spain, as well as voices from places such as Africa (via the slave trade), the Middle East, and Asia. In Argentina as elsewhere in Latin America, that Spanish affinity had begun to clash with a mainstream culture increasingly shaped by a more cosmopolitan, and also urban, working-class European immigration.

The plains cattle driver has always been a marginal figure, and he has always survived under threat of extinction. From the beginning, his cultural expression has been ready for a hard ending. So, when the postmortem mythologizing began, the nostalgic pall cast over his image was intricately tied to the fact that he was already gone and deliberately reconstructed in the glow of hindsight. This accounts for the tone common to both the later gauchesque and the US Western genres: there is, everywhere, a heartbreaking and elegiac lyricism projected onto the landscape.[6] A line from a review of the Western film *Seraphim Falls* (2006) summarizes what could be nearly a century of this convention: "The severe beauty of the Western landscape looms over the characters as a silent rebuke" (Holden E23). The gaucho's post-Edenic mythology, always predicated on a sense of its own ending, leads to what the Argentine critic Josefina Ludmer calls a double emphasis of the gauchesque genre: both "challenge"—the gaucho's hardscrabble combativeness—and perpetual "lament." The lament is built into the genre itself, as Ludmer has powerfully argued.[7]

In their central and quite prominent place within the national imaginary, both the range driver and the gaucho are creatures that have always been out of place—first because of their outlaw nature and later because they exist "after the fall," caught in their own representation, their own posteriority. The moment the cowmen are conscripted into a stylized form at the service of others—be that the gauchesque or the Western—they disappear. They cannot, and will not, lose their freedom to roam, even when they *do* lose it: "Gauchos are free, courageous, landless men who must be respected. They refuse to submit, to serve, defending this liberty with the law of courage. . . . Thus they appear forced to remain outside the law" (Ludmer 134). This interesting contradiction about both sets of horsemen is that, when they become part of national projects that extend beyond their "endless plain" and are drafted into a mythical origin story, they are paradoxically doomed to both disappear and live on forever. The open-range horseman is most useful to the metropolis as a missing subject, captured at the moment and place of his disappearance. As Ludmer says, "There is a use in the differential voice of the gaucho" (20).

Still, we must not forget that the range horseman's true calling is to roam in freedom, endlessly unconstrained on the open sea of green, for he has no fixed home. The "silent rebuke" of the landscape's "severe beauty" tells of this conundrum, which raises a much larger question: Can the unfettered, free-roaming America(s) that the horseman supposedly embodies achieve full agency and representation when this embodiment is artificially captured—conscripted—in that post-traumatic form and genre? If the untamable wilderness that germinated North American individualism, ingenuity, and Emersonian self-reliance, as well as the *criollismo* that is at the deepest root of Latin America, is at risk of being tamed, can it be freed again through an invented version, be that the gauchesque or the Western? The very notion of "Americanness" is at stake. When gauchos fall into the gauchesque and cowboys into the Western literary and film genre, the result is a crisis of representation and a paradoxical fixity, an unwanted permanence.

A Partnering Moment of (F)light

> This man had saved his life, which was something; but, further, he was the ideal master.
> —Jack London, *The Call of the Wild*

In a brief story called "The Biography of Tadeo Isidoro Cruz," Borges rewrote the climactic moment of *Martín Fierro,* when Cruz defects from his military unit. As the title announces, the tale is told from Cruz's perspective rather than Fierro's. It is another outlaw gaucho's life story from the moment of his conception at that very homestead, after which his own father was also surrounded by a troop and killed in battle. Years later the attempted arrest of Martín Fierro occurs in the same spot, but now Cruz defies repetition and rises to join forces with the outlaw Fierro and help him defeat the posse. The reason Cruz defects is his sudden realization—not of the coincidence of finding himself in the place where he was conceived, but of *all* the fateful parallels, the seemingly inescapable homologies, including the one between himself and Fierro: "Once fully understood, that night encompasses his entire story—or rather, one incident, one action on that night does, for actions are the symbol of ourselves. Any life, however long and complicated it may be, actually consists of *a single moment*" (213).

As Borges points out, awareness of this inescapable sameness, the single moment, leads to a moment of insight about one's fundamental nature. And that insight comes from recognizing oneself in someone else who is identical: suddenly finding a homologous other. Cruz sees himself in the mirror of one more cornered gaucho like so many others, and this recognition of kinship finally prompts him to act in a way that doesn't even require words in order to happen—it can't *not* do so. Cruz has suddenly found an ally with whom to fight, someone who is another version of himself. Immediately after the fight, the pair sets out for the wilderness. This is an acceptance of the Nietzschean eternal return: the inevitability of sameness makes both men stronger, able to venture out for years on end.

In *The Searchers,* after the Comanches kidnap the girls, the party that rushes out to find them initially consists of several men but gradually dwindles to just three: Ethan (John Wayne), the uncle of one of the captive girls and an avowed Indian hater; Martin, who might have Indian blood and is the adoptive brother of the girls; and Brad, fiancé of one of the captives. Ethan catches up to the band of Indians, reconnoiters their camp, and is obviously troubled by something he has seen. He goes to meet the others. They have also seen the Comanches from a different vantage, and this exchange takes place:

BRAD (*shouting it*)
  I saw her! . . . I saw Lucy!
  . . .

ETHAN (*voice flat*)
  What you saw wasn't Lucy.

BRAD
  It was, I tell you!

ETHAN
  What you saw was a buck wearin' Lucy's dress. . . . (*they stare at him*) I found Lucy back there in that canyon. . . . I wrapped her in my blanket an' buried her with m'own hands. . . . I thought it best to keep it from you—long as I could.

(*He can't look at Brad or at Martin. Brad can't speak—and then finally:*)

BRAD
  Did they . . . ? Was she . . . ?

(*Ethan wheels on him in shouting fury.*)

ETHAN (*blazing*)
What've I got to do—draw you a picture? . . . Spell it out? . . . Don't ever ask me! . . . Long as you live don't ever ask me more!

(*Brad wipes his mouth with the back of his hand. He turns—walking stiff-legged as though on stilts back to his horse. He bends his head against the saddle, as though to hide his grief. Martin turns away.*)

Brad goes mad with rage, jumps on a horse, and singlehandedly charges the Comanche camp in a suicidal attack. Ethan keeps Martin from joining him.

(*The distant yammering of the Comanches doesn't quite drown out one stifled scream of pain; we can surmise a scalping knife was busy in the last instant of Brad's life. Martin slumps in his saddle. Ethan listens a moment, then turns to Martin.*)

ETHAN
Let's just hope he took some with him.

(*He turns his horse back the way they had come. Martin stares at him.*)

MARTIN
What you goin' to do?

ETHAN
Get some sleep. . . . Tomorrow's another day.

This shocking act of violence produces as little expression in Ethan as in Fierro, sauntering to his horse after killing a man. They have lost one of their own, and Ethan and Martin's posse finds itself reduced to two, without much comment—"Tomorrow's another day"—like the night Cruz wordlessly joins Martín Fierro. They have been silently reduced to the pair of fellow searchers of the film's title, forming an unlikely alliance, since Ethan is an Indian hater and deeply suspicious of Martin. But they have so much else in common that they will embark on their shared search through the wilderness, mile after mile. *For years.*

Whatever else has thrown the two pairs together—necessity, fate, the inevitable circularity of events—Cruz and Fierro and Ethan and Martin are inextricably linked by similarities stronger than anything that makes them different. These similarities, in the face of such enormity, fashion their foregone alliance. It happens wordlessly. The perfunctoriness, the inevitability of such a union, is natural, given the steady and silent rhythms of this way of life. When one spends hour after hour on the back of a horse, there is nothing to break up one's thoughts or the solitude except the constant rhythm, one hoofbeat exactly like the other. That interminable and constant rhythm becomes part of you: it leads to a kind of measured self-possession that extends to everything, even to pulse-raising punctuations like stampedes, Indian attacks, or a killing. This lies behind the tacit inevitability of their long-term similarities. Riding is what they were doing anyway, silently and endlessly, and would have continued doing, whether just to reach someplace to "get some sleep" before setting off on yet another day's ride or to fight once more—singer against singer, range rider against the weather or an Indian, gaucho against gaucho. It almost doesn't matter what the battle is, or whose side they're on. Acting at a moment of mutual recognition, a pair suddenly forms, wordlessly nodding in acknowledgement of their common nature—and they just keep moving. This moment of homology provides clarity: the range driver *sees* and recognizes his own situation in someone else. He finds it natural to join his double—his fellow—as a silently acknowledged partner, to keep going with few words exchanged with this natural extension of himself.[8]

In Annie Proulx's gay-themed story "Brokeback Mountain" (1997), two seasonal range workers ride together one summer, tend a flock on a mountainside, and fall in love with one another. Many years later, when Ennis del Mar learns that his erstwhile lover Jack Twist has been killed, he repeats to himself a refrain of resignation, well worn by years of repressed desire: "There was some open space between what he knew and what he tried to believe, but nothing could be done about it, and if you can't fix it you've got to stand it" (269). Stoic open-range horsemen like Martín Fierro or Ennis del Mar "stand it"—ironically, by *not* standing still but by setting out yet again, almost endlessly, through the vast and open spaces.

In the years after their initial encounter while herding on Brokeback Mountain, Ennis and Jack find a way to get back together every so often. They take off on long, meandering trips away from their wives and families, ostensibly to fish and hunt. They try to recapture that first summer on the mountain when they found love for each other. In the narrative, these secret encounters are reduced to a lyrical list of place names: "Years on years they worked their way through the high meadows and mountain drainages, horse-packing into the Big Horns, the Medicine Bows, the south end of the Gallatins, the Absarokas, the Granites, the Owl Creeks, the Bridger-Teton Range, the Freezeouts and the Shirleys, the Ferrises and the Rattlesnakes, the Salt River range, into the Wind Rivers over and again, the Sierra Madres, the Gros Ventres, the Washakies, the Laramies, but never returning to Brokeback" (271). Their trips away from the normativity of their settled lives and into the vastness of the land amount to an intermittent attempt to repeat, and preserve, that first moment of mutual recognition on the mountain when they fell into each other's arms with a wordlessness that made it seem inevitable:

> Nothing he'd done before but no instruction manual needed. They went at it in silence except for a few sharp intakes of breath and Jack's choked "Gun's goin off," then out, down, and asleep.
>
> Ennis woke in red dawn with his pants around his knees, a top-grade headache, and Jack butted against him; without saying anything about it, both knew how it would go for the rest of the summer, sheep be damned. As it did go. They never talked about the sex, let it happen. (260)

Although this is the first homosexual encounter for both of them, there is something familiar, natural, and seamless about their mutual recognition, "no instruction manual needed." Their unexpected encounter emerges because of the fundamental similarities in just about everything else about this pair. At the beginning of the story the narrator introduces them with a single, shared description, separated only by a bit of geography: "They were raised on small, poor ranches in opposite corners of the state, Jack Twist in Lightning Flat, up on the Montana border, Ennis del Mar from around Sage, near the Utah line, both high-school drop-out country boys with no prospects, brought up to hard work and privation, both rough-mannered, rough-spoken, inured to the stoic life" (254). Ennis and Jack are versions of same "rough-mannered, rough-spoken, stoic" person, with one perhaps more volatile than the other. This homology makes them look for the same thing: himself *in* the other.

After that summer together on Brokeback, Ennis and Jack meet for the first time under new terms. Both are now married to women and have started lives away from the wide, lyrical expanses of time and landscape that enabled their first encounter. They flow into each other's arms again with an unscripted naturalness: "They seized each other by the shoulders, hugged mightily, squeezing the breath out of each other, saying son of a bitch, son of a bitch. . . . Still they clinched, pressing chest and groin and thigh and leg together, treading on each other's toes until they pulled apart to breathe and Ennis, not big on endearments, said what he said to his horses and daughters, 'Little darlin'" (264). Their mode of connection, their frame of reference, consists of those things they have had in common: horses, and now children. And, since their recent domesticity featuring wives and daughters is something they could never have shared with each other off the range, they return to the range for the only thing they *can* share: meandering horseback trips, hunting and fishing instead of herding stock.

Homology is a powerful attraction. The reason a range driver can easily slip into being an outlaw is that the life of the outlaw isn't that different from his life as a cowhand, at least terms of what is experienced and required daily: the endurance, the wilderness skills, the absence of law, the slow constant motion, the indifference to danger, the achingly beautiful and vast expanses. The everydayness is the same; you have to keep moving for endless miles through the land, stopping occasionally for food and rest and staying alert to the known dangers, and then getting up and doing it again. Whether the range driver (or the gaucho) rides the range to push steers or to avoid the law, it's pretty much the same to him. It means a whole lot of ground to cover. These rides were measured out not with coffee spoons but in days, months, even years.

In the time between the "Departure" and the "Return" of *Martín Fierro,* when Cruz and Fierro venture into the true wilderness as fugitives, their adventure goes "off-camera." We don't see or hear much about what happens in the Indian territory, or even how they manage to survive. When they enter this narrative gap they leave behind the semisettled expanses where the law—still somewhat sketchy and in its infancy—is taking firmer hold. When they do return, the law is much more present than before, and it has become clear that their previous ways are no longer possible. The wilderness had provided them with a reprieve from time, serving as a prenormative territory, like psychoanalyst Julia Kristeva's concept of *chora,* a primal and preverbal space (25–30). As the old chestnut goes, history is really just one damn thing after another. The true wilderness is ahistorical because it lacks such a predictable sequence—lyrically so, in the case of Ennis and Jack's attempt to stop the entropy of time in order to preserve their love. It is also where another pair of white, outlaw men on horseback can disappear and where progress, and the law, cannot follow.

One of the most haunting episodes in Alvar Núñez Cabeza de Vaca's *Narrative* of his 1527 wilderness journey through the US South and Southwest is a brief, easily overlooked passage, where when he stops traveling and "spen[ds] in this land" some time alone among the natives: "The reason I stayed so long was to take with me a Christian who was on the island, named Lope de Oviedo. . . . In order to take him out of there, I crossed over to the island every year and begged that we go, in the best manner that we could, in search of Christians. And every year he kept me from going, saying that we would go the following year" (98). He periodically goes to bug the other survivors to go back on the road with him. Then Cabeza de Vaca simply sums his existence up: "The time that I spent in this land, alone among them and as naked as they, was nearly six years" (98). *Six years:* this significant portion of his life is written off in one brief sentence, stoically, even casually.

In the "Return" of *Martín Fierro,* when the gaunt outlaws Cruz and Fierro reemerge at a *pulpería* after a very long time out in the desierto, there is little to say about those lost years. That time is gone, without much fuss, like the uncommented-on life of the mulatto whose blood Fierro nonchalantly wiped from his blade while sauntering back to his horse. What happens in the true wilderness is blank, unwritten. It isn't even history: it doesn't warrant as much as a section of a backcountry gaucho ballad. The essential "cowboyness" of these fleeing pairs is reconfigured, each in its own way, during their interludes in the lawless wilderness.

But, when they return from the true wilderness, what is waiting for them is backcountry, where the rule of law is more and more present. They face the disappearance of their original way of life, with skills that are a better fit for less settled environments.

A Third Will

Gender theorist Eve Kosofsky Sedgwick observes that intense male relationships are never just about the pair, that there is always something more bringing them together. Invoking French philosopher René Girard's notion of triangular desire, she argues that close male affective relationships, even those that aren't necessarily erotic or sexual—"homosocial"—are mediated by some third element, some shared desire or impulse. Sedgwick surveys literature of the eighteenth and nineteenth centuries for a list of some of these common, mediating third wheels: competition over a woman who is "symbolic property" (26); homophobia (what she calls "homosexual panic") that ironically drives men together; or, in some cases, sublimated homoerotic desire that can't be acted upon directly and thus needs to be recast in other terms.

This third intervening element can also be a sociopolitical pressure, a permeating reality as large as empire. Sedgwick makes an elaborate case for the Gothic novel as such an example where "class difference"—another common third element in male homosocial relations—is replaced by a much more charged form of class difference, an Orientalizing "fantasy-prone distinction between the domestic and the exotic," created by the vast overseas empire ruling over a world of otherness. She gives the example of British traveler, adventurer, and scholar Richard Burton, famous for translating *The Arabian Nights* into English and for traveling in native drag. Burton argued for the existence of a geographic "Sotadic Zone": a longitudinal ring close to the equator, where permissiveness thrives and immoral practices like pederasty are practiced by the locals as "mere peccadillo." When the "civilized" white male, the northern colonial interloper, ventures into this charged zone, he can find himself infected and "'go[es] native': there is a taint of climate" (161). However, what happens in the Sotadic Zone doesn't stay in the Sotadic Zone. When the colonizer returns home, he brings with him its influence to bear on his love interest there, creating a triangle in the closed Gothic spaces at the heart of empire. These imported habits reflourish far from the cooler metropolis, in hot, dusty places where no one sees or cares—much like the ways of the open-range rider. As Josefina Ludmer writes, "Gauchos are free, courageous, landless men who must be respected. They refuse to submit, to serve" (134).

The vast plains of open-range grazing "zones," North and South—Borges's lands of the "Indian, the lasso, the wild horse"—are often cast in nautical terms, as oceans of green, or *mar verde* (*Poems* 207). They offer a sense of interminability. Like the ocean, these expanses are places of isolation, repetition, and few witnesses. Individual actions seem insignificant, and "a man's cry dies a lonely death." An unspeakable injustice committed here, two hundred and eleven miles ridden there, a score settled somewhere else, endless nights under the stars—all these things will go on somewhere on the plains, equally unremarked upon. When things get tough out there, you just "stand it."

The stoic relationships that emerge between paired rangers who navigate these expanses together reflect the power of that endlessness, where time and life don't leave much of a mark. But perhaps the herders' strongest relationship is with the environment itself, as an element of their togetherness. There couldn't be a closer relationship than the one between the range rider and that enormous and achingly beautiful landscape, because that rider has no homestead—he is "landless," as the anti-gaucho laws of vagrancy pronounced. He has no *plot:* no story that links him to a delineated parcel of land in the settled sense. At the conclusion of all these narratives, the pairs are bound to split up. The contrast between the range riders' way of life, with its hermetic isolation, naturally and tonally fits with an awareness of the coming end. When Ennis del Mar visits Jack's grave, the lyrical "silent rebuke" of the "grieving plain" itself is a projection of the pair's doomed wanderings—interminable and timeless at one point, but no longer (Proulx 282).

In the moment of recognition when each of these pairs forms, the range rider suddenly realizes that he's not alone and has found a traveling companion—and this traveling companion is as doomed as he is. A natural, almost unacknowledged, partnership falls into place. It will give both of them a last chance to share a home on that range. And that traveling home is partly possible because of the recognition of a dying homology. Their silent togetherness will provide only a temporary measure of comfort, a kind of domesticity that extends the everydayness they have always known and helps them "stand it," if only for a while. The constant, forbidding enormity and endlessness afforded by the land is coming to an end; Ennis and Jack would "never return to Brokeback."

3 The Size of Domesticity 1
Traveling Companions Flee from Cold War "Containment" in *On the Road* and *The Motorcycle Diaries*

> Rise up in birth with me, my brother.
> From the deep zone of your wide-spread sorrow give me
>   your hand.
> —Pablo Neruda, "The Heights of Macchu Picchu"

AT THE conclusion of George Roy Hill's 1969 Western/buddy film *Butch Cassidy and the Sundance Kid,* the pair of outlaws has this exchange in the middle of their last gun battle:

> BUTCH: I got a great idea where we should go next.
> SUNDANCE: Well, I don't wanna hear it.
> BUTCH: You'll change your mind once I tell you—
> SUNDANCE: Shut up.
> BUTCH: Okay, okay.
> SUNDANCE: It was your great ideas got us here.
> BUTCH: Forget about it.
> SUNDANCE: I never want to hear another one of your great ideas, all right?
> BUTCH: All right.
> SUNDANCE: Good.
> BUTCH: BUTCH: Australia.

During this scene the character of Sundance (Robert Redford) takes a cloth from his pocket and almost absentmindedly wraps the wounded hand of his partner, Butch (Paul Newman). This moment of tenderness conflates two fights happening of very different scales: a massive shootout to the death, and the long-running spat between men who have been traveling together, perhaps for too long. In the middle of a desperate battle against an overwhelming force, their petty domestic squabble finds an intimate little truce. Like many mainstream cultural products from the

1950s and 1960s, this film is an appropriate allegory of the tensions of the Cold War. A pair of men, closely bound and on the run, find themselves surrounded by forces much, much larger than they.

Their plight is a familiar one; tales of pairs on the road proliferated during the high Cold War, defined roughly as the period from the end of World War II to the late 1960s. Some of these traveling pairs were seeking something, others running away. Notable examples include Vladimir Nabokov's novel *Lolita* (1955) and Dennis Hopper's film *Easy Rider* (1969), whose protagonists embark on road trips to distance themselves from the standards of the time, in order to engage in things they really shouldn't. Their escape fantasies highlight the sharp normativities and anxieties of the period.

Arguably the most representative narrative of this very American kind of tale is Jack Kerouac's 1957 semiautobiographical novel *On the Road*. This work and the many that followed its contours—what became the American road genre—are so tied to the specific context of the US Cold War that it is somewhat remarkable the genre traveled to other times and places as well. But the road genre *did* travel—to Latin America, for example. Before examining this strange migration, we should outline the uniquely North American specifics of the genre, its shape and sources, in order to highlight the peculiarity of its transcultural passage.

The novelist Thomas Pynchon recalls his time as a beginning writer during the late 1950s: "I think, looking back, that there might have been a general nervousness in the whole college-age subculture. A tendency to self-censorship. It was also the era of *Howl, Lolita, Tropic of Cancer*, and all the excesses of law enforcement that such works provoked" (xiv). The postwar economic boom in the United States provided a robust consumer society and a sense of economic security. But this prosperity found itself at odds with the constant insecurity posed by the Soviet menace, creating W. H. Auden's "Age of Anxiety."

The cognitive split between material comfort and the ever-present threat of annihilation led to an unprecedented psychic tension. It also generated an intense culture of normativity, intended to calm and domesticate the tension and the paradox that was generating it. The clichéd characterization of the 1950s is one of generalized numbness, as laid out in the 1959 poem "Memories of West Street and Lepke" by the confessional poet Robert Lowell. The poet pads around in his pajamas, institutionalized and sedated:

> These are the tranquilized *Fifties*
> and I am forty.
> Ought I to regret my seedtime? (85)

Lowell's verse captures the unreal, sedated quality of that period after the war. What should have been a well-earned and placid middle age is instead filled with incapacitating anxieties and regrets. A suffocating sense of confinement and an awareness of artificiality define the time: "tranquilized," yet not peaceful. The knowledge that everything could be blown up at any moment induces a localization and an internalization, a turn from the epochal ("These are the tranquilized *Fifties*") toward the deeply personal ("I am forty"). It is a survival tactic against the pressure.[1]

This complex, almost universal, response—a psychosocial and cultural analogue to the political and military strategy adopted in response to the Soviet menace—led to what Cold War scholars such as Alan Nadel and Elaine Tyler May have labeled "containment culture." According to them, containment was the overarching narrative for the period as well as its master trope. An extensive body of scholarship argues that containment shaped the US national imaginary and inflected just about every level of discourse, public and private. The simplistic binary of "us" against "them" became an almost overwhelming paradigm and metaphor, and ultimately its simplicity provided a regulatory tool for many long-standing and completely unrelated social tensions.

Nadel examines how the stark global East/West response to the Soviet "other" was easily superimposed onto many internal "enemies." This Cold War dualism was conveniently invoked as a disciplining shorthand for many other conflicts: the witch hunts of McCarthyism and the House Un-American Activities Committee persecuting popular culture; the response to the civil rights unrest of the period, which identified the "upstart Negro" with communism because both were simultaneously visible and invisible; the terms of perversion and promiscuity that framed discussion (and prosecution) of sexual "deviances" in ways usually reserved for the Soviet enemy.

This stark polarization also laid the groundwork for the societally forced normalization of the "good": the mythology of the middle-class nuclear family living a serene existence in sharp disregard of the threats from outside. Leading a calm, comfortable life was the best form of defiance. "Normal" life would stave off the looming threat. This was not a case of mass delusion; everyone knew that not all was perfect. In fact, the superficially placid domestic narratives of 1950s normativity led to momentary eruptions of all sorts, unhealthy aberrances lurking in plain sight. But these would only be defeated by that aggressive normalcy, the rule of the domestic. As May writes,

> In the domestic version of containment, the "sphere of influence" was the home. . . . Within its walls potentially dangerous social forces of the new age might be tamed so they could contribute to the secure and fulfilling life which postwar women and men aspired. Domestic containment was bolstered by a powerful political culture that rewarded its adherents and marginalized its detractors. More than merely a metaphor for the Cold War and the home front, Containment aptly describes the way in which public policy, personal behavior, and even political values are focused on the home. (16)

For our purposes, a key aspect of Cold War containment is its size, its sense of scale—or, rather, the two scales that coexisted simultaneously: one, the small and inward-looking refuge, and the other a vast, global, threat. As May puts it, the "large, multifarious, national policies became part of the cultural agenda" of "ordinary citizenry," people living their daily comfortable and materially secure lives (8).[2]

The immediate response to the insecurity of the time was a retreat to the space of the well-off middle-class family, and a "parlor aesthetic." The tract-housing living room, bourgeois good taste, and explicitly apolitical forms reigned, resisting the underlying global tension through domestic "tranquility." This inward-looking normativity was the American version of central European Biedermeier, the hermetic culture of middle-class gentility that pervaded polite society just after the horrors of the Napoleonic Wars, when the Austrian Empire's Chancellor Metternich ruled repressively over an affluent but tense peace. Neoclassical simplicity and sedate tonality dominated. Of this period and its aesthetics James Sheehan says, "In contrast to public culture, the private sphere was familiar rather than monumental, enclosed rather than open, inward looking rather than expansive. For the private sphere, people wrote piano solos rather than symphonies, designed villas rather than public buildings, did family portraits rather than official statues. This was a domestic world furnished with sideboards and comfortable chairs, filled with painted porcelain" (535–36). That European period of relative wealth and intense conformity produced complicit self-censorship—just as Pynchon recalls about the 1950s. There was a universal unwillingness to dissent from the official culture, concentrating instead on the comfort afforded by the new prosperity. There was little motivation to acknowledge the internal or external pressure, lest that ruin everything for everybody. The memory of recent horrors—be they the Napoleonic Wars or World War II—kept everyone complicit with the charade. This domestic peace, however, could not continue unchallenged. A restless youth would rise up—in the revolutions of 1848 in Europe, and in the 1960s in the United States.[3]

After a rending world conflict, the United States in the late 1940s and 1950s was looking inward, to the comfort of close familial proximity. Like Biedermeier's turn toward the ephemeral—light verse, tasteful interior design, and gossamer parlor music—the North American middle class turned to the hearth. Television and movie escapism ruled; Disneyland opened its fantasy doors in 1955. When families forayed outside of their homes, they carried that world along with them. Mobile homes were the rage. Road vacations along the new Interstate Highway System were made quite easy in the powerful family car—now within the acquisitive reach of the middle class—a portable, tailfinned microcosm of the family home.

Concentrating on what was supposedly stable—the nuclear family, the economy, material ease—made emotional sense, given the conflict in the air. The retreat into domestic spaces, of course, didn't mean that either the conflict or its shadow had been banished from those comfortable spots. But acknowledging it would have meant giving in to it, and the fear of what everybody knew was there was sublimated into the available aesthetic and social forms. Fallout shelters were a version of the repressed fears. Manicured domesticity offered a counterbalance to the lurking sources of tension, large and small.

A Return Home

The speed of geopolitical rearrangement after 1945 is striking but logical. The immediate shift from hot war to Cold War required a new mentality and an attendant language. Winston Churchill was one of the defining voices of both conflicts. During the darkest moment of World War II, in his "Finest Hour" speech to Parliament (1940), he famously laid out the scale of the conflict by invoking the personal places where the desperate struggle would need to happen: "We shall fight on the beaches, we shall fight on the landing grounds, we shall fight in the fields and in the streets, we shall fight in the hills; we shall never surrender" (316).

But just six years later, on March 5, 1946, when the hot war was over and won, Churchill issued his "Iron Curtain" speech defining the terms of the new Cold War. He laid out how radically everything had changed, and he inaugurated the rhetoric that would accompany this new conflict. The terms are familiar, similar to his earlier speech: once again he invoked a juxtaposition of the small and local with the large. But now this was far more dramatic. In the 1946 speech—nominally about the "special relationship" between the United States and Great Britain—he described the new enemy in terms of what would be required of those fighting it: "The safety of the world, ladies and gentlemen, requires a [new] unity in Europe, from which no nation should be permanently outcast. . . . Twice the United States has had to send several millions of its young men across the Atlantic to fight the wars. But now war can find any nation, wherever it may dwell, between dusk and dawn" (7289). Inaugurating the cooperative internationalism that would soon split the world in two, Churchill hinted at an intimate sense of place and home, the "dwelling" of an entire community of nations. The newly awakened Soviet foe, replacing the recently defeated fascists and their crudely geographic and material ambitions, was a much larger and darker threat, an idea bigger than simple imperialism. And this idea could lurk everywhere and anywhere in the new, vast, indefinite space-time "between dusk and dawn."

Countering this new idea, this enemy-as-abstraction, required a new sense of temporality and an attendant psychology, but, most important, a new sense of the enormous differences in scale. Instead of the physical beaches, streets, hedgerows, and massive mobilizations of World War II, the new battlefield would be intangible, located in the even more contained space of one's own head. But a largesse was also required, said Churchill, and a largeness: a "new unity," a grandness of all like-minded nations that would form a kind of nurturing global family "from which no nation should be permanently outcast," a welcoming domesticity of the like-minded, at once enormous and intimate.

This intensifies the dichotomy already present in the earlier hot-war rhetoric. In the new locus of conflict, it would be up to individual citizens to make the difference on the small scale. The key to victory would be in close quarters—the only available place to defeat the enormous threat. The stakes of this asymmetrical relationship could not be more pronounced. The threat of global annihilation—the fate of everything that mattered to all humanity—would be settled in local spaces, putting put those small places under a warning that they were on the front line, and an immense amount of pressure.

Hence the sense that in postwar America the retreat into the normalized, suburban refuge was, even more than a duty, a heroic gesture. The identical walled havens of the Levittown suburbs offered a fractal version of the besieged nation. Picket-fence fortresses contained tiny multitudes and kept out the hordes. On a small scale, they stood in for the war against the enormous intangibles, be those communistic, racial, sexual, or affective.

US diplomat George Kennan's "Long Telegram" to the state department from Moscow in 1946, later echoed in an article he published anonymously in *Foreign Affairs* magazine, is a foundational text of the Cold War, because it set out to define the "Soviet psyche." It emphasized how the United States needed to show constancy and restraint—self-containment—in order to triumph over the Soviets' undisciplined, almost lewd aggression. The communist Russians, Kennan argued, were counterpointed by an equally virile but disciplined United States, while the Soviets were unable to contain their "vital fluids" (39). They were bad *men*.

Masculinity and the kinds of relationships through which men could relate to each other were also redefined under the pressures of the Cold War. Another influential essay from this period, "Come Back to the Raft Ag'in, Huck Honey!" (1948) by American literary and cultural critic Leslie Fiedler, explores a consistent thread in American literature: a pattern of male escape. Focusing on what he calls "boys' adventure stories" by writers such as James Fenimore Cooper, Herman Melville, and Mark Twain, Fiedler connects this pattern to two contemporary "deviances": Blackness and homosexuality. According to Fiedler, those who identified with and lived out lives within those labels were forced into an in-house, accounted-for marginality; they had to adapt to a role of recognizable otherness within the normative culture. The characters in the works Fiedler studies took to the road to escape the enforced binary of their condition by making them unlocatable: as travelers, they were no longer "one of those" people. Reflecting the Cold War pressures of the time, Fiedler implies that the titular normativity of gender and race was everywhere and shaped everything, and that it was hard to escape. But some tried (670–71).

This idea extends into an interesting implication about what was specifically *not* the norm—the counterculture—and about the pressures that drove it during the 1950s. One common reading about the era is that its rebels, its restless young men, were simply responding to the suffocating normativity and generalized anxiety through forms of delinquency. But, given the relative comfort and prosperity of the period, this delinquency was relatively small, attention-seeking gestures, often focused on individual, if vibrant, representatives—the iconic rebels—rather than on movements (even the civil rights movement can be read this way); think of Marlon Brando, James Dean, Elvis Presley, Rosa Parks. Among these individual-scale objectors, seekers, and dropouts were the Beats and the jazz musicians of the Benzedrine-driven bop they listened to, the rock-and-rollers, and the daring iconoclasts of the early civil rights movement. These heroic, mercurial figures were out to reject the normalcy of the time. Pynchon recalls trying to become a writer in the shadow of the Beats:

> Like others, I spent a lot of time in jazz clubs, nursing the two-beer minimum. I put on hornrimmed sunglasses at night. I went to parties in lofts where girls wore strange attire. I was hugely tickled by all forms of marijuana humor, though the talk back then was in inverse relation to the availability of that useful substance. I already knew people who would sit in circles on the deck and sing perfectly, in parts, all those early rock'n'roll songs, who played bongos and saxophones, who had felt honest grief when Bird and later Clifford Brown died. . . . When the hippie resurgence came along ten years later, there was, for a while anyway, a sense of nostalgia and vindication. Beat prophets were resurrected, people started playing alto sax riffs on electric guitars, the wisdom of the East came back in fashion. It was the same, only different. On the negative side, however, both forms of the movement placed too much emphasis on youth, including the eternal variety. Youth, of course, was wasted on me at the time. (xiv)

These 1950s "dropouts" were quite oppositional but also localized, functioning as sharp but relatively individual—contained—exceptions, always on a small scale. They were, as Pynchon writes, explicitly *not* like the massive and collective expressions that would come later, in the 1960s and 1970s.[4]

The intimacy of the mainstream "containment culture" seems to have carried over into its escapees and rebels, whose rebellion included a turn toward closeness. In the case of Kerouac's *On the Road,* the smallness of middle-class life couldn't contain Sal Paradise, so he chose another smallness, one that was on his own terms: on the move. One way to read *On the Road* is as a dispatch by the malcontents of empire telling the mainstream to bug off. But another is to read it as a story of those malcontents as refugees, who, in a way, find a place of their own that is really not so unlike the home that they've fled. They are looking for the same, only different.

This dynamic is visible to someone like Pynchon, who arrived at the alternative scene just too late. Seeing it in the rearview mirror can explain its fundamental nature: "Eventually as post-Beats [we came] to see deeper into what, after all, was a sane and decent affirmation of what we all want to believe about American values" (xv). Pynchon confirms that these localized rebellions—these little 1950s escapes from little places into similarly little places—are actually "a sane and decent affirmation" of exactly what these rebels were pretending to leave behind. They were simply trying to find a hearth of their own, their version of that little household, on the move. As critic Kris Lackey notes, Kerouac's book is "a novel of little households and big highways" (138).

Two Vastnesses

> You must know that I do not love and that I love you,
> because everything alive has its two sides.
> —Pablo Neruda, "Love Sonnet XLIV"

Like the original picaresque initiated by the *Lazarillo de Tormes,* discussed in chapter 2, *On the Road* is predicated on a deep but oddly nihilistic determination to live fully and at all costs to overcome a stiflingly bad situation. Another connection to the picaresque is Benedict Anderson's attraction to the genre as a useful tour d'horizon by outsiders looking in, as explored in his *Imagined Communities*. These travelers' revelations ring true precisely because they are compromised, or at least ambivalent. They are also critical and blunt, but still complicit with the project of empire. Told by a hardened outsider, the picaresque eyewitness account can be critical while at the same time functioning as a corroborating instrument. *On the Road,* like the *Lazarillo de Tormes,* offers unvarnished dispatches from the margins of empire, and it depicts the places that set those limits: roadside diners, racially edgy jazz clubs, reform schools, hospitals, bohemian hangouts with their puerile intellectualism, migrant worker camps, amphetamine "connection" bars, places of commerce both legal and illegal, and Mexico. The reports about these places can easily be read as celebratory of what they are not (the mainstream) and emancipatory, as vibrant exceptions. Or they can be seen as places with which the travelers, gladly, do not form a permanent bond. Perhaps they are both.

There is a continuity linking these places. At the start of the book, Sal Paradise writes about the terms of his trip with Dean: "I first met Dean not long after my wife and I split up. I had just gotten over a serious illness that I won't bother to talk about, except that it had something to do with the miserably weary split-up and my feeling that everything was dead. With the coming of Dean Moriarty began the part of my life you could call my life on the road. Before that I'd often dreamed of going West to see the country, always vaguely planning and never taking off. Dean is the perfect guy for the road" (3). Sal takes off to replace the disaster of his youthful marriage. He substitutes a new and exciting relationship, deeply alive, for the just-ended one that had nearly killed him. But despite the frenetic, Benzedrine-driven appetites driving this new trip, it mimics the ideal of what it proposes to leave behind, shaped by the need for intimacy and domesticity, for the model nuclear family. Despite the adamant insistence on constant mobility and the implied promise of freedom, the travelers set out within a parallel "little household" reformulated as a portable—and masculine—domesticity. If one squints hard enough, it becomes clear that the pair of road travelers looks like the "normal" families they have so emphatically left behind.

The domesticity of their breakout is, like everything else touched by the Cold War, a conflation of scale. To reprise Eve Kofsosky Sedgwick's observation that homosocial relationships are triangular and include a complicating, outside element that ultimately binds men together (as discussed in chapter 3), the road genre's homosocial third element is the enormous nation that they power through—the backcountry roadsides of (mostly) the South and the West, the "coldwater flats" of its cities, the deserts and migrant camps. This vast, scrolling reality stands in sharp relief against the smallness of their "little household" (Lackey 138). And the contrast bestows an epic quality upon their story. As Kerouac would later write about the goal of his trip, "Dean and I were embarked on a journey through post-Whitman America to find that America and to find the inherent goodness in American man" (Leland 17). To find a generalized quality, an inherent goodness: this deceptively simple desire takes the mitigating factor in Sedgwick's homosocial triangle to an enormously wide angle, to the scale of the entire national landscape and its universal "goodness." Vastness is the road genre's essence—but paradoxically, so is intimacy.

This gets more interesting. The story of restless young men taking to the road to discover the "real" country—actually escaping and being with each other in an attempt to refashion the unacceptable intimacies from which they've escaped—is deeply tied to a specific waypoint, the Cold War in the United States. Yet the genre traveled on to other places. "Road" works have flourished in Latin America. Recent examples include Chilean novelist Roberto Bolaño's *The Savage Detectives* (1998), Mexican director Alfonso Cuarón's film *Y Tu Mamá También* (2001), and the short story and related graphic novel *Road Story* (2007) by Chile's Alberto Fuguet, a prominent member of the post-Boom's "McOndo" generation of younger writers who reacted to it. But the most insistent champion of this genre in Latin America has been the Brazilian film director Walter Salles, whose passion for the road runs deep. Salles even directed the first cinematic version of *On The Road* (2012).[5] His most interesting conversation with the US road genre, though, is his film *The Motorcycle Diaries* (2004), chronicling the real-life trip of the young Ernesto "Che" Guevara, the future revolutionary, and his traveling companion, Alberto Granado. Their journals and letters from 1952 provide the narrative basis for the film.

The voyage of the road genre to Latin America raises the question of just how dependent this master narrative is on the specific context of US postwar prosperity and American empire at a particular high point in history. The objects of desire generated by the United States (a prosperous but encircled nation, and the resulting intimist Biedermeier-like culture) would logically be quite different from the social and political contexts of Latin America. So, how does the road genre, so inextricably shaped by its time and place, carry through to Latin America, with its entirely different political circumstances and social realities—even reverse ones, given Latin America's position relative to the United States?[6] Asked more simply, what happens when this quintessentially North American master narrative—young men searching for themselves (and each other) via road trips through the heart of empire—transmigrates onto another landscape, equally enormous but vastly different (if still American)? *Latin* America is quite pointedly not empire, and if anything, it is the *subject* of empire.

In Latin America, the road genre finds itself redeployed to times and places that are explicitly *not* at the heart of empire: Argentina, Chile, and Peru of the early 1950s (and by superimposition the 1990s and 2000s, when Salles' movies were filmed). Do the resonances, contours, and anxieties that framed this narrative at its source travel with it? A partial answer: the juxtaposed scales—the ratios of the story, and the ratios of desire—remain basically unchanged, but what is contained in these scales is not. And thus the resulting stories, anxieties, and travels are ultimately different, if proportional to each other.

The fundamental difference between the two journeys—Kerouac's and Guevara's—is what each pair of travelers sees "out there," and how that relates to the homes they left behind. Although the natural vistas the Argentines saw from their motorcycle were as vast and breathtaking as any Sal and Dean would have seen through their windshields and Greyhound bus windows, Ernesto's South America would have been quite different from the United States, at least in terms of the poverty on view as they traveled. The urban Argentina of Córdoba and Buenos Aires, where Alberto and Ernesto began their trip, was essentially first-world in 1951. But from there, they traveled into a stark and progressively racialized third world, into a kind of poverty deeper than any in the United States—or at least what Sal and Dean were able to see of it.

During the seventy years before Ernesto and Alberto's trip, Argentina had achieved unprecedented economic growth and reached social stability, fueled by an enormous tide of European immigration that swelled the metropolitan centers, from 37 percent of the population in 1895 to 63 percent in 1947 (Anderson, *Che* 29). Steady development, guided by a series of more or less democratic governments, had begun slowing down during the Great Depression and World War II (military dictatorships and labor unrest had started creeping in). But when the populist Juan Perón came to power in the 1940s there was a temporary reprieve to the decline. The Peronista government was strong-armed, corporatist, and protectionist. By the early 1950s, when Ernesto and Alberto abandon their studies and their place in the Argentine middle class to take off on their trip, that middle class was relatively safe—especially in comparison to the rest of South America. Urban Argentina in 1950 was still by far the richest place on the continent. The young men's path away from Buenos Aires follows a trail of incremental poverty, starting in Chile. The display of inequality reaches its climax in Peru, where the per-capita GDP in 1950 was roughly half that of Argentina.[7]

By contrast, while Sal and Dean do see economic inequality—one of Sal's stops on his initial trip in 1947 is to pick cotton in a Mexican migrant camp in California—they seem to skim past it, always remaining at a distance. During their second trip in 1949, from North Carolina via New Orleans to San Francisco, they roar through the bayous:

> "Man, do you imagine what it would be like if we found a jazzjoint in these swamps, with great big black fellas moanin guitar blues and drinkin snakejuice and makin signs at us?"
>
> "Yes!"
>
> There were mysteries around here. The car was going over a dirt road elevated off the swamps that dropped on both sides and drooped with vines. We passed an apparition; it was a Negro man in a white shirt walking along with his arms up-spread to the inky firmament. He must have been praying or calling down a curse. We zoomed right by; I looked out the back window to see his white eyes. "Whoo!" said Dean. "Look out. We better not stop in this here country." At one point we got stuck at a crossroads and stopped the car anyway. Dean turned off the headlamps. We were surrounded by a great forest of viny trees in which we could almost hear the slither of a million copperheads. The only thing we could see was the red ampere button on the Hudson dashboard. Marylou squealed with fright. We began laughing maniac laughs to her. We were scared too. We wanted to get out of this mansion of the snake, this mireful drooping dark, and zoom on back to familiar American ground

and cowtowns. There was a smell of oil and dead water in the air. This was a manuscript of the night we couldn't read. An owl hooted. We took a chance on one of the dirt roads, and pretty soon we were crossing the evil old Sabine River that is responsible for all these swamps. With amazement we saw great structures of light ahead of us. "Texas! It's Texas!" (169)

The "apparition" of the "Negro man" is not much more than a puerile prank to spook a girl. Despite the thrill of possibly discovering "a jazz-joint" with "great big black fellas moanin guitar blues," the swamp and its "slither of a million copperheads" is a place they'd rather not get out of the car to see. They remain in their little moving home until they reach their next safe little island, a more recognizable Texas of (white) diners, cities, and country fairs, and on to the next apartment of someone from their small but spread-out circle of like-minded youth rebels. They will make stops with their friend Bull Lee, or with one of Dean's wives, or some other friend from the jazz underground.

"This was a manuscript of the night we couldn't read": the vastness is illegible to them—and exciting—but that illegibility tightens their focus to their little portable space. The only thing they could see was a tiny point of light, the "red ampere button" inside their little car/living room. For Sal and Dean, the allure of the landscape's enormity and variety serves both as an object of impossible desire and as a foil, a contrasting counterpoint to their own close-quarters erotic attraction for one another. These complicated erotics are just as inexpressible as the vast land, and just as incomprehensible to those watching them closely—the women they've abandoned in their confining domestic situations:

> I learned that Dean had lived happily with Camille in San Francisco ever since that fall of 1947; he got a job on the railroad and made a lot of money. He became the father of a cute little girl, Amy Moriarty. Then suddenly he blew his top while walking down the street one day. He saw a '49 Hudson for sale and rushed to the bank for his entire roll. He bought the car on the spot. . . . Now they were broke. Dean calmed Camille's fears and told her he'd be back in a month. "I'm going to New York and bring Sal back." She wasn't too pleased at this prospect.
>
> "But what is the purpose of all this? Why are you doing this to me?"
>
> "It's nothing, it's nothing, darling—ah-hem—Sal has pleaded and begged with me to come and get him, it is absolutely necessary for me to—but we won't go into all these explanations—and I'll tell you why. . . .No, listen, I'll tell you why." *And he told her why, and of course it made no sense.* (110–11, my emphasis)

Dean told her "why," but readers never get to hear that why—only, gleefully, that it made no sense.

The almost nonsensical imperative to get out there on the move, to find "that America," becomes a perpetual postponement of meaning, a sort of excuse to prolong their time with each other. The enormity of one side of the triangle—the vast "America"—is what makes that possible. It extends the trip, hopefully indefinitely. This is similar to how literary critic Paul de Man defines irony: "Permanent parabasis," in which a Greek chorus' meandering asides to the audience become the narrative itself, the new constant (*Blindness* 228).

Their road trip is also a running postponement of the pull of the normative. The massive asymmetry within the road relationship is unsettling and exhilarating, and yet ultimately it repeats what's waiting back home. Another way of considering this is via a phenomenon observed by postcolonial theorist Leelah Gandhi, about the unusual friendships that can happen between the colonizer and the colonized. In what normally would be a vastly unequal relationship, a bond of "philoxeny" is formed, based on mutual impetus for reinvention of a relationship, by forcing a "cultivated *ataraxia,* or invulnerability, and *autarkia,* or self-sufficiency" (29).

The bond in *On the Road,* while not between colonizer and subject, is predicated on a massive asymmetry in the triangle of desire. Given the enormous size of one angle, that boundless landscape, it is certainly a "cultivated ataraxia," and "autarkia." The smallness of the portable home stands in sharp contrast with the entire "sad American night," a deliberately interminable object, the end of which can't be fathomed even after days of continual driving: "O sad American night! Then we were in New Mexico and passed the rounded rocks of Raton and stopped at a diner, ravingly hungry for hamburgers, some of which we wrapped in a napkin to eat over the border below. 'The whole vertical state of Texas lies before us, Sal,' said Dean. 'Before we made it horizontal. Every bit as long. We'll be in Texas in a few minutes and won't be out till tomorrow this time and won't stop driving. Think of it'" (156).

Just as it did for the cowboys and the gauchos, the whole of America stands as a constant reminder of the pair's fundamental pressure-tightness, the smallness of their little space in contrast with the world through which they traverse. In unequal relationships, says Gandhi, the asymmetry of the "local or global" is "emotionally risky." And journeys into asymmetry lead to unexpected places: they result in reinvention. (In *The Motorcycle Diaries,* reinvention will be the case with Ernesto's political awakening, soon to turn him into "Che.") *On the Road* is both the story of a reinvention of domesticity, via detour—through a resizing of its triangularity—and the story of Sal's own reinvention, as a writer. In *The Motorcycle Diaries,* these stories transmigrate into a story of political reinvention. This is not to say that *On the Road* isn't political, but it doesn't tell the story of a *political* awakening.

In a psychoanalytic comparison of *On the Road* and *The Motorcycle Diaries,* the critic Josefina Saldaña Portillo makes the compelling case that the distinction between the two sets of travelers is that Sal's trip represents unresolved melancholia for the lost object—the "already lost ideal of white freedom"—whereas Ernesto *becomes* a "textbook example of successful mourning." Saldaña Portillo argues that this is because Ernesto's observations are those of a trained physician who is developing a political "diagnostic function"; he has an eye for injustice and "constantly historicizes, contextualizes, analyses and draws conclusions" (92). Sal, on the other hand, simply "fetishizes impoverished racialized subjects as the condition of possibility for his white freedom" (100). But Saldaña Portillo concludes that ultimately both trips are centered on the loss of an abstraction, the racialized other, that ultimately translates into an egotistical instrument of self-affirmation. Although Ernesto's engagement with that self-confirming other might be more socially aware than Sal's, Saldaña Portillo maintains, it still amounts to no more than "great, grave, dead Indians" whose admiration for the lost Inca empire was because it had "resisted the colonizing Spaniards unto death" (102). In other words, on the road, boys can't help being boys: their quixotic searches are quests by the heroes and warriors of Empire.

I would disagree with this reading, given the vast difference in the territories of the two trips. While I agree that both sets of travelers are inward-looking and their journeys are ultimately self-confirming, there is a larger sociohistorical difference at hand to consider.

Empire without Empire

Despite the formal similarities between *The Motorcycle Diaries* and *On the Road,* the backcountries through which they take us are very, very, different. Naturally the trips produce different results. The narrative of *The Motorcycle Diaries* is driven by its off-camera future: Ernesto and Alberto will evolve from young, adventurous students into world-changing revolutionaries. Everyone knows that is coming and their road story serves as an explanatory backstory. The afterlife of the Argentines' trip both reinterprets and extends the story of Sal and Dean.

The Argentines' road trip is informed by two important textual works. The first is the *Canto General* by Chilean poet Pablo Neruda, a collection of Petrarchan love songs addressed to the landscape—to the physicality of the continent and its history—expressed in terms of bodily desire. It is a Whitmanian celebration, or, as one critic has phrased it, the "erotics of geography." The second is the *Seven Interpretative Essays on Peruvian Reality* (1928) by the Marxist theorist José Carlos Mariátegui. Neruda's book serves as a useful tool for the pair of travelers. Ernesto was fond of quoting this well-known poetry to girls (Anderson 36). Neruda's poetry is something Ernesto carries with him from home; the poet's Romantic, breathtaking visions of the Americas spurred the travelers' imagination about what they would see. Indeed, the trip was partly plotted on the cartographic flow in the sequence of poems. The film, just like the book of poems, climaxes with an emotional visit to the ruins of Machu Picchu; the cornerstone poem is "The Heights of Macchu Picchu."

The book by Mariátegui, on the other hand, is something they discover out there, once they are on the road. In Peru they are generously taken in by Dr. Pesce, a socially conscious physician who runs a leper colony in the backcountry. The good doctor offers them "food, clothes, and some very good ideas," as Ernesto says in a letter to his mother (heard in voice-over in the film). Pesce hands Ernesto a copy of *Seven Essays,* a book previously unknown to him. Looking up from it, he exclaims in wonder that "Mariátegui talks about the revolutionary potential of the natives and farm workers of Latin America. He says that the problem of the Indian is the land and that the revolution should not be an imitation. It should be original and indigenous" (170). Then the film switches to a scene of what director Salles has called the "documentary" perspective of *The Motorcycle Diaries,* which consists of actual interviews with present-day, nonactor indigenous subjects, filmed in black-and-white. Although these scenes are anachronistic and break the narrative frame, they are meant to be representative of the people the travelers would have encountered ("Notes" 67).

Ernesto's minimal summary of *Seven Essays* is fairly accurate, but there is a nuance to take into account. Mariátegui was an unusual Marxist in that he was deeply committed to the "telluric," the specific here and now of the land, which he believed should not be ignored in the class struggle. He also felt that employing the ideas of international Marxism to fix the problems specific to Latin America, and explicitly those of Peru, could dilute that local perspective. The standard international model of proletarian empowerment could easily miss the unique relationship existing between the Peruvian people and their specific place. Mariátegui wrote extensively about that link, focusing on his interpretation of the indigenous notion of *Tawantinsuyo*—both a religious code and a concept of oneness with the earth. He argued that Tawantinsuyo could be the atavistic "moral" force to counter the imperialistic "theocratic" Incas, and the Spanish Catholic institutions that replaced them (146–68). Mariátegui invoked the prehistory of the indigenous population in his treatment of their current impoverished condition, concluding that a true revolutionary solution required returning to the links with the land. This, in turn, would lead to a home-grown recovery of the means of production: class struggle would come from within, through a return to the way things had been before Inca and European conquest, long before any Enlightenment notions of industrial-age revolution had forgotten this pastoral source. In a way, Mariátegui proposed Marxism without Marx, an "original and indigenous" Marxism.

Mariátegui's practical proposal for land reform was to break up *gamonalismo*, the system of haciendas and monopolies, and to replace it with individual, family-plot farming within a collective framework, guided by the collectivizing spirit of Tawantinsuyo. This would require communal ownership and consultative decision-making: avant-la-lettre sustainability, employing long-established technology that can only happen at a small scale, via mutual agreement and shared ownership.[8]

Mariátegui's idealistic and idealized plan for local indigenous revolution resonated with the young Ernesto. Mariátegui offered a way for him to understand what he had been seeing in the vastness of his trip, visions that had deeply affected him but required unpacking. He needed a way to understand the specific, racialized, desperate poverty afflicting the Latin America he was witnessing for the first time. What Mariátegui proposed for Peru, his brand of reverse-engineered Marxism, was a retreat into little homesteads. Ernesto felt the resonance of this proposal within himself.

Ultimately the resort to the small-scale solution in the middle of an engagement with something breathtakingly and seemingly unsurmountably large extended to Ernesto the revolutionary. The principal philosophy of Che Guevara, of the man he would become, was known as *foquismo*—a military and doctrinal strategy of independent operation by highly mobile revolutionary cells, or *focos*. In his manual on guerilla warfare he writes how "each guerrilla fighter carries his complete equipment" and is capable of operating for an indefinite period away from the main forces (85). As a result, "the nomadic life of the guerrilla fighter in this stage produces . . . a deep sense of fraternity" among his small group of travelers operating independently (89). These groups would operate almost like families on the move, carrying everything they needed on their backs. And the monumental undertakings that would result would be made possible by the intimacy that originated in their travels, a sustaining bond that would lead to bigger things.

4 The Size of Domesticity 2
Subcomandante Marcos's On-the-Run Dispatches Repurpose Cold War Anxiety

> The national sovereignty resides essentially and originally in the people. All public power originates in the people and is instituted for their benefit. The people at all times have the inalienable right to alter or modify their form of government.
> —Article 39 of the 1917 Constitution of Mexico, as amended in 2010

> I'm a pessimist because of intelligence, but an optimist because of will.
> —Antonio Gramsci, "Letter from Prison," December 19, 1929

WE COME to an interesting supplement to the Cold War, where enormity again encounters smallness and where fellow travelers negotiate both gradations. This played itself out just after the Cold War was technically over, and not on the global stage, but in the middle of nowhere—in the backcountry—during a small indigenous revolt in Mexico. The Zapatista uprising of 1994–96 offers another wandering interconnection between North America and Latin America.

A much-anthologized jungle communiqué by rebellion spokesman Subcomandante Marcos, dated March 11, 1995, was composed in the midst of a hasty retreat from a military crackdown. The circumstances were these: after the initial uprising of January 1, 1994, there had been nearly a year of tense peace. The far-superior force of the Mexican federal forces poised to annihilate the poorly armed rebels had decided to pull out its troops and allow the insurgents a small region of semiautonomy—mostly because of the vast public outcry generated by Marcos's widely circulated Internet communiqués. But, in 1995, all of this changed.

In the middle of the prolonged negotiation between the Zapatistas and the government, the Mexican Army was brought in to take back the area. In his lengthy communiqué, written in the frenzied style that would become his hallmark, Marcos wove revolutionary slogans and demands, straightforward news from the front, and fanciful narratives. As had become the norm for his writing, this one went viral in various Web and print venues. In this particular communiqué, Marcos tells how he and two other colleagues are engaged in a "strategic withdrawal"—which, he grudgingly admits, really means they are on the run, fleeing for their lives, as the army chases them through the jungle (see fig. 6).

As Marcos relates it, one morning while setting up camp (he and his comrades sleep during the day so they can travel at night to avoid detection), he almost steps on an insect. This cartoon-like beetle, Durito, or "little hard one," would soon become his frequent interlocutor, a fellow traveler and sidekick. After nearly being crushed, it takes a while for the bug to calm down and recognize the masked man, whom he now remembers from before he became an officer. Durito, prickly fellow, gives Marcos some friendly grief, sponges some tobacco off of him, and asks about his current plight. They are, Marcos admits, on the run.

The year 1992 had been symbolic for North America in terms of its world importance. It was the quincenteary of the arrival of Columbus in the New World. More important, it was the year that the major North American economies—the United States, Canada, and Mexico—signed the North American Free Trade Agreement (NAFTA), widely condemned

Figure 6. On the run. *Sucomandante Marcos* (*Subcommander Marcos*), 1994. Photograph by Antonio Turok. (Collection of Antonio Turok)

by the Left as a tool of US economic imperialism. According to this view, the treaty meant the most significant move away from local interests and toward an unequal, globalized economy on a par with the advent of the European Union. As Michael Hardt and Antonio Negri argue in their book *Empire* (2000), virtualizing the location of the means of production—a "non-place"—offered a new way of sublimating ownership and furthering class war (208–10). An organized resistance to this orchestrated grand gesture away from the local and toward the global was not surprising. What *was* surprising, at least in Mexico, was that the embodiment of this resistance was the small and very local conflict by the Ejército Zapatista de Liberación Nacional (EZLN).

This ragtag movement, with its recycled uniforms and barely functional weapons, at first blush seems like a familiar fixture from Latin America's long history, almost a throwback: a land-reform peasant uprising with racial underpinnings. The name "Zapatistas" itself invoked indigenous revolutionary leader Emiliano Zapata, a land-rights fighter during the disastrous Mexican Revolution of 1910–25. It could easily be grouped with the Cuban Revolution–inspired Central and South American movements of the 1970s and 1980s, such as the Nicaraguan Sandinistas (also named for a previous revolutionary icon) or the Peruvian Shining Path.

Yet, during the initial stages, the Zapatista rebellion announced a much larger project attached to its armed insurrection. It aimed to become an international pressure organization against the forces of globalizing neoimperialism. The date chosen for the actual military uprising clearly illustrated this double agenda: January 1, 1994, was when NAFTA went into effect. The uprising's push for wider relevancy—its antiglobalization angle—brought with it an unprecedented new battleground. When the Zapatistas launched their bullets-and-bombs attack on local military garrisons, they also invaded the Web in an assault against free-market trade agreements.

This double mission was clearly embodied in the EZLN's equally unprecedented choice of spokesman—the anonymous and masked "subcomandante," nom de guerre Marcos. Clearly an educated and urbane mestizo and not a member of the indigenous population for whom he was fighting and speaking, Marcos unleashed an eclectic torrent of erudite communiqués, postings, emails, and other creative output. These showed a comfortable engagement with classic Marxist and Latin American revolutionary discourse, a keenly ironic voice, and a mastery of the short forms required by electronic media, and made knowing references to both high and popular culture. Many surprised members of the world media called him the first postmodern revolutionary.

Of course, when the educated mestizo Marcos became the public persona of the indigenous rebels, it raised a lot of complicated questions about racial and class identity, authority, legitimacy, ventriloquy, and appropriation, not to mention rhetorical strategy.[1] Marcos claimed that his main role was to educate outsiders, or become an *intérprete,* as he often called himself. His role, he said, was that of a methodical, deliberate teacher. The figure of the teacher is everywhere in Marcos's considerable output, especially in the initial years of the rebellion (1994–96). There is "Old Man Antonio," a shamanistic indigenous character who shares his ageless wisdom with Marcos; the arrogant beetle Durito, political expert and traveling companion; and Marcos himself (real name Rafael Sebastián Guillén Vicente, he had been a professor at the Universidad Autónoma Metropolitana). A vital function of these teachers was to educate the rebels themselves: Marcos often shows them explaining the nature of the enemy to the troops. And one consistent aspect they keep hammering home is the link between the local aims of the rebellion and global causes. There is a clear connection between the frightfully immediate and the looming, perhaps more frightening, global implications of the struggle.

Marcos's double-voiced version of Zapatismo both channels and refashions an unusual source: the culture and poetics of the 1950s, the "high" Cold War, explored in the previous chapter. Both the high Cold War discourse and Marcos's teacherly figures voice the calming certainty of victory in the face of an overwhelming new enemy—a reassurance, a deep belief of being on the right side. The academic exudes moral certainty, despite the awareness (real or contrived) of being embattled and even surrounded. The circumstantial elements of these two discourses—on the surface quite distant from each other and perhaps even diametrically opposite—share more than appears at first blush.

As discussed in the last chapter, anxiety about encirclement at the highest point of the world conflict led to "containment culture." As historian Alan Nadel details, the foreign policy task of containing the enemy—Soviet expansionism—was profoundly echoed in the prosperous, consumerist, but ultimately stifling cultural containment of the time. I do not suggest that this Western bourgeois phenomenon was the exact response of the Zapatistas; rather, there is a striking similarity in how both discourses respond to a sense of siege—of being encircled by an overwhelming enemy—and invoke similar strategies in their widely different contexts. Both force a tense, eye-of-the-storm peace; both resort to "placid" domesticity, sometimes to the point of infantilization; and, most important, both elevate hieratic figures, often academics, to explain the desperate times. As Che Guevara wrote in his manual on guerrilla warfare:

> The organization, combat capacity, heroism, and spirit of the guerilla band will undergo a test of fire during an encirclement by the enemy, which is the most dangerous situation of the war. In the jargon of our guerrilla fighters in the recent war, the phrase "encirclement face" was given to the face of fear worn by someone who was frightened. The hierarchy of the deposed regime pompously spoke of its campaigns of "encirclement and annihilation." However, for a guerrilla band that knows the country and that is united ideologically and emotionally with its chief, this is not a particularly serious problem. (*Guerrilla* 90)

The professorial aspect of Marcos's persona makes sense given the announced goals of the rebellion, which frankly needed a little explaining. But his double role can sometimes come across as jarring, if not contradictory. A spokesperson educating the public needs to offer a consistent front; he is there to explain, to sell the aims of the revolution. But this often stands at odds with the role of the representative leader: someone who must encompass both his followers and his skeptics, collectively and democratically, via engagement and charisma, using humanizing, individual examples.

Marcos's double-tasked shaman-professor is a new kind of emitter of dispatches from the backcountry. He attempts to explain resistance against the metropole to (mostly) educated observers watching from the outside. But the frame narrative, the conceit he uses to do so, is to present scenes of teaching, of providing strength, to his less-educated fellow fighters. Marcos's teachers explain to the public, through their explanations to the troops, the reasons behind the fight, which provides a deeply necessary encouragement to the combatants themselves. The function of a wartime professor is to decipher the essence of a supposedly inscrutable enemy. To his fellow travelers/fighters, he is a hieratic figure, the confident possessor of privileged knowledge about the enemy. And he often implies—and sometimes says outright—that this knowledge is the key to victory. His knowledge is certainty.

Marcos's double discourse is natural, given the double nature of the Zapatista uprising itself, at least in its initial years. Scholars Herman Herlinghaus and Kristine Vanden Berghe have each argued that the one struggle gradually transformed into the other out of necessity. After the initial defeat, the armed struggle was replaced, in vastly different terms, by a larger and more indefinite struggle that had worldwide significance.

These scholars observe in the language of the revolt a progression from the traditional dead earnestness of the anti-imperial revolutions of the past—Cuba, Central America, the Peruvian Communist Party (Shining Path)—to a more playful, ironic, and literary tone, as it moves toward the larger and more indefinite arena of cyberspace and into the unquantifiable space of postnational global politics.

The Mexican intellectual Carlos Fuentes famously called Zapatismo the "first post-communist" rebellion.[2] But, at least initially, both straight-ahead Marxism and post-Marxism existed in an almost schizophrenic alternation. Consider the straightforward language in writings like the "Primera declaración desde la selva Lacandona," which earnestly quotes Article 39 of the 1917 Mexican Constitution, guaranteeing the right of an aggrieved people to rise up in arms against an unacceptable government. Contrast this with the fanciful and provocative stories featuring Durito or Old Man Antonio, or personal vignettes about some of the guerillas. These two registers exist in an oddly eclectic flow.[3] Yet despite the technical and stylistic novelty of Marcos's discourse from these early years, with its command of new media and high irony, it still relied on familiar Marxist tropes and is informed by a typical Latin American Marxist critique of the effects of domination at the individual level. Marcos's bifurcated discourse during these initial war years appears to be an internal contradiction within a single teacherly voice—a traveling self-dialogue. His voice is at once local and global, speaking both to the guerillas gathered around him and to a much larger listening audience.

In the communiqué of March 1995, Marcos explains to Durito why he finds himself on the run at that particular moment. On the way to the negotiation conference, the Mexican government had been informed when to expect the delegates, and it used this information to mount an attack. Marcos was able to escape with two fellow guerillas:

> Durito went on smoking, and waited for me to finish telling him everything that had happened in the last ten days. Durito said: "Wait for me." And he went under a little leaf. After a while he came out pushing his little desk. After that he went for a chair, sat down, took out some papers, and began to look through them with a worried air. "Mmmh, mmh" he said with every few pages that he read. After a time he exclaimed: "Here it is!"
>
> "Here's what?" I asked, intrigued.
>
> "Don't interrupt me!" Durito said seriously and solemnly. And added, "Pay attention. Your problem is the same one as many others. It refers to the economic and social doctrine known as 'Neoliberalism.'"(53)[4]

The conversation leaps from three insurgents fleeing through the jungle in a desperate attempt to save their skin to a detailed explanation of that global threat of "Neoliberalism." This points to the well-documented mid-1990s paradox at the heart of Zapatismo itself: it is double-voiced. This discourse, especially as expressed by Subcomandante Marcos, is simultaneously global and profoundly local, and personal.

In the encounter with Durito, we see a clear manifestation of how Marcos approaches his double mission. What do you do when you are under hot pursuit, terrified that the surviving few are about to be overrun by the enemy? *You teach. About big things.* Che Guevara again, on individual guerrilla tactics:

> The education of the guerrilla fighter is important from the very beginning of the struggle. This should explain to them the social purpose of the fight and their duties, clarify their understanding, and give them lessons in morale that serve to forge their characters. Each experience should be a new source of strength for victory and not simply one more episode in the fight for survival.
>
> One of the great educational techniques is example. Therefore, the chiefs must constantly offer the example of a pure and devoted life (89).

In the jungle narrative, Durito pulls out his desk and his papers and begins to explain the whole situation in terms of an abstract concept: neoliberalism. One can imagine him wiping the blackboard, or setting up a PowerPoint presentation. Marcos reacts understandably to this arbitrarily enforced lesson (as perhaps many of his readers do as well): "'Just what I needed . . . now classes in political economy,' I thought. It seems like Durito heard what I was thinking because he chided me: 'Ssshh! This isn't just any class! It is a treatise [cátedra] of the highest order!'" (90). The Spanish word *cátedra* is significant here; it refers both a lecture and the physical place of the lecture, the professor's "chair" (a double meaning to which I will return later). In any case, a pattern emerges: the local and pressing battle sublimates into a vast, abstract war of ideas. This scene of teaching in the heat of a local engagement is meant to be seen—and disseminated—on a much larger scale.

We can look to the culture of the Cold War for insight into the sort of relationship that can occur between the small-scale, domestic front and a much larger global standoff. Both Marcos's discourse and the Cold War culture come at a time of crisis created by the threat of an inscrutable and enormous enemy, and both look toward a teacherly figure who must carry out multiple roles to counter that threat. Before World War II, US administrations including Franklin Delano Roosevelt's had drawn heavily for leadership from professional politicians, the party faithful, and an experienced, select few from business and industry. Academics had been called upon as experts, typically in advisory roles; if they had actual leadership positions where they could effect policy, it was because of a previous administrative track record that had effectively been a career change, as was the case with Woodrow Wilson. They stopped being sages and became leaders and politicians.

But, in postwar administrations, beginning with Harry Truman's, there was a clear turn toward technocracy, toward handing actual decision-making authority to the authorities. In order to fill important economic, scientific, intelligence, diplomatic, and policy positions, a new breed of leaders was recruited directly from the academy, based primarily on knowledge rather than any sort of practical government experience. These men had not typically risen through the traditional political ranks but, rather, belonged to the most elite universities and think tanks. This trend culminated in John F. Kennedy's idealistic but misguided "best and the brightest" coterie of policymakers—men such as Arthur Schlesinger and McGeorge Bundy, who eventually shaped the disastrous Vietnam War policy.

During the Cold War, this turn toward technocrats was largely due to a pressing need that only they could fill. For one, the high-tech nature of nuclear armaments required unusual scientific expertise. But, most important, the communist Russians were deeply unknown, to the point of abstraction and inscrutability, and required expert decipherment. The "new professors" were there to make them less imposing. Because they had gained their insight into the Russian mind the hard way, often learning the language in a vacuum and scrounging as much information as they could about a closed society, the Russia experts achieved a role that went far beyond that of mere specialists; these Cold Warriors were defenders of the capitalist faith. And, like any priestly figure, they had attained this position by having a reach to unseen forces that extended beyond the grasp of the average coreligionist.

Recall Winston Churchill's opening rhetorical salvo of the Cold War mentioned in the previous chapter, his "Iron Curtain" speech of March 5, 1946: "Twice the United States has had to send several millions of its young men across the Atlantic to fight the wars. But now war can find any nation, wherever it may dwell, between dusk and dawn" (7289). The enemy is as pervasive as the morning light, and all legitimate democracies need to unite against this new foe. When Churchill delivered this speech, it was not to a political body—not to the British Parliament, the US Congress, or the United Nations. Instead it was to a rather intimate academic audience at Westminster College, a small liberal arts school in Missouri. Churchill was wearing professorial garb appropriate to the honorary degree he was being awarded, presaging the coming ivory-tower technocrats, the "best and the brightest" tapped to lead the country through the conflict. Also recall American diplomat George F. Kennan (one of those best and brightest), who wrote another foundational text of the Cold War, the "Long Telegram" sent to the state department from Moscow in 1946. He then fleshed out his views in a 1947 *Foreign Affairs* article under the mysterious mask of "Mr. X." The spirit of these documents—Churchill's and Kennan's—would shape the Truman Doctrine and subsequent anti-Soviet policy for decades. "[The Soviets'] success will really depend on the degree of cohesion, firmness and vigor which Western World can muster" (16–17), Kennan wrote, implying that the enemy is incoherent, amoral, and flaccid, ultimately doomed, but only if "cohesion, firmness and vigor" are maintained effectively in the face of this looming threat.

This is not unlike the oddly optimistic Professor Durito, who ignores the dangerously close Mexican Army, pulls out his little desk and papers, and expounds professorially from his cátedra about the enemy. But, according to him, the enemy is not the Mexican soldiers (or the Soviet menace), but rather the looming specter of neoliberalism:

> "It is a metatheoretical problem! . . . Well, it turns out that 'Neoliberalism' is not a theory to confront or explain the crisis. It is the crisis itself made theory and economic doctrine! That is, 'Neoliberalism' hasn't the least coherence; it has no plans or historic perspective. In the end, pure theoretical shit."
>
> "How strange . . . I've never heard or read that interpretation" I said with surprise.
>
> "Of course! How, if it just occurred to me in this moment!" says Durito with pride.
>
> "And what has that got to do with our running away, excuse me, with our withdrawal?" I asked, doubting such a novel theory.
>
> "Ah! Ah! Elementary, my dear Watson Sup! There are no plans, there are no perspectives, only i-m-p-r-o-v-i-s-a-t-i-o-n. The government has no consistency: one day we're rich, another day we're poor, one day they want peace, another day they want war, one day fasting, another day stuffed, and so on. Do I make myself clear?" Durito inquires.
>
> "Almost . . ." I hesitate and scratch my head.
>
> "And so?" I ask, seeing that Durito isn't continuing with his discourse.
>
> "It's going to explode. Boom! Like a balloon blown up too much. It has no future. We're going to win" says Durito as he puts his papers away. (53–54)

Because the neoliberal Mexican government is reactive, devoid of "plans," and incapable of true insight, Durito concludes (with the inevitability of a true believer) that, despite the incredibly long odds, the besieged rebels will win. Both George Kennan and Durito characterize their looming enemy as "improvisational" and "not schematic," essentially an instinctual and unreflective creature, like some overgrown lower-order organism. It effectively manages its colonizing mission by mindlessly regulating its own survival functions, keeps all its moving parts moving; it will respond only to significant changes in its environment, or to irritation.

A Mouse's Tour d'horizon

It is difficult to argue for a direct analogy between the anxieties of the US high Cold War and Marcos's brand of Zapatismo—after all, they belong to opposite sides of the political spectrum. They are obverse in both scale and function, but the correspondences are there. A somewhat facile parallel could be drawn with the semiautonomous enclave of the "five towns" that the Mexican government allowed to exist during the first three years of the Zapatista uprising, while negotiations were ongoing. This enclave, understandably, existed in an anxious sense of siege: a bizarro Levittown.

But the link runs deeper. During the 1950s there were sharp outbreaks of actual "hot" war in Korea and Vietnam, but for the majority culture in the US the Cold War was a distant rumble. It involved an edgy public trusting the informed few to maintain a deep, schematic, and theoretical knowledge about the enemy and its methods in order to forestall total annihilation. The rank-and-file population's fight was mental. It consisted of keeping anxiety at bay and staying one step ahead, heartened by a fierce faith in the inevitability of success: Kennan's call for "cohesion, firmness and vigor."

The main strategy was to staunchly maintain everydayness, to keep doing what one always did, to demonstrate grace under pressure. The enemy was so large and so myopic that ultimately it would trip itself up in the face of this constancy. The strategy was steadiness in the face of the Other's "improvisation." This imperative toward enforced everydayness held true whether the enemy was Stalinism or, in the case of Marcos, the Mexican Army in particular and neoliberalism in general. Recall the duality within Marcos's discourse about strength in the face of the enemy: some of it is for internal consumption, its intended audience his fellow *camaradas,* and some of it is meant for the outside world. The complicating factor is that within that larger message is inscribed the image of Marcos—the teacher, cheerleader, prophet of certainties—telling his fellow combatants on the ground how to win this mental war. This is an integral part of the message projected to the world at large. Marcos *shows* the rebels learning about and thus winning the mental war over anxiety, if not the real war against the government. This is shrewd recycling of Cold War methods and modes of thought. When Marcos's performative (and teacherly) discourse channels these coping mechanisms and refashions them for his immediate struggle, it brings us to two specific strategies used effectively during the Cold War: simplistic "children's" narratives and masked superheroes.

During a particularly difficult time for the Zapatistas in the late 1990s, Marcos went oddly silent, leading to intense speculation that he had been killed or captured, or that he had given up the struggle for some reason. Then he suddenly returned to the fray with a memo titled "Subcomandante Marcos Breaks Silence after 4 Months" (July 15, 1998):

> To: The Mexican Federal Army
> The Guatemalan Army
> Interpol, Paris
> CISEN [The Mexican Center for Research and National Security], Polanco
>
> Sirs:
>
> > Eepa, eepa, eepa!
> > Andale, andale!
> > Arriba, Arriba!
> > Eepa, eepa!
> > > —From the mountains of southeast Mexico, Insurgent Subcomandante Marcos (Alias "Sup Speedy Gonzalez," or what amounts to "a thorn in the side"). (Ejército Zapatista de Liberación Nacional Mexico, et al., 195, my translation)

This, of course, is a reference to popular Warner Bros. cartoons of the 1950s. Besides playing with the racial stereotype of a character like Speedy, Marcos invokes the cartoons because of their central place in the culture of the Cold War. The reference is so familiar that Marcos can rely just on Speedy's signature interjection: he only needs to repeat the nonsensical "Eepa, eepa, eepa!" for readers to make the connection.

A curious connection, this is. The apparently lighthearted cartoons of the 1950s were tied to the anxious gravity of Cold War psychology.

During that decade an important state project was spreading the gospel of free-market economics as the only viable alternative to communism. As the animation historian Steven Watts has written, the massively popular, optimistic worldview offered by cultural institutions like the Disney studios "legislated a kind of cultural Marshall Plan. They nourished a genial cultural imperialism that magically overran the rest of the globe with the values, expectations, and goods of a prosperous middle-class United States" (107). Another significant voice in this globalizing task was the Alfred P. Sloan Foundation (created by the longtime president of General Motors) which disseminated the capitalist gospel through more traditional venues; it funded academic research, cultural outreach, and educational and commercial exchange programs, both domestically and abroad. It also paid Hollywood studios to produce popular films to aid its efforts.

Among these was a sequence of three animated films commissioned from the Warner Bros. animation outfit. Issued as part of the very popular *Looney Tunes* series, these were made in the standard six- to seven-minute formula and tapped established stars such as Sylvester the Cat and Elmer Fudd. "By Word of Mouse" (1954), "Heir Conditioned" (1955), and "Yankee Dood It" (1956), all funded by the Sloan Foundation, were directed by the legendary Isidore "Friz" Freleng. The initial setting of "By Word of Mouse" is the postwar German town of "Knockwurst-on-der-Rye," where a large German mouse family begs Hans to tell everyone about his recent trip to America. His country-mouse/city-mouse tale begins with Hans disembarking from an ocean liner and meeting his American friend Willy, who agrees to take him on a tour of the splendors of the land.

The fellow traveling mice visit the sights of the great city, and Hans—impressed by the number of cars and other consumer goods—exclaims that all Americans must be rich. Willy corrects him. "They're not all rich. Most of 'em are just working guys," he says. When Hans asks how "working guys" can afford such luxuries, Willy struggles to explain mass consumption and production, and economies of scale. He gets nowhere. So he takes Hans to Putnell University, where he hopes a mouse professor can clarify the concept of free-market capitalism. The professor gladly attempts to explain and pulls out a series of flip charts. But in the middle of his lesson about mass production lowering costs and competition nurturing innovation, Sylvester the Cat appears out of nowhere, sees them, and thinks of lunch. The bulk of the cartoon consists of the three mice fleeing the cat, trying to find places to hide and continue their ersatz economics lesson. They escape into the drawer of a filing cabinet (see fig. 7), then a desk drawer,

Figure 7. Still from *By Word of Mouse,* directed by Friz Freleng (5:12)

and finally a paper boat floating inside the water-cooler bottle. Each time Sylvester finds them the professor foils him—by slamming drawers on him, pummeling him with a hammer, or making him fall down a manhole.

In the end Hans finally understands the concept of free markets, but he also decides that, given the pursuing cat, the situation has become just too dangerous for him. He goes back to the ocean liner to return to his Marshall-plan homeland. After making Sylvester fall down a hole one last time, the professor shouts after the hurrying Hans, "Don't forget! All of this has raised our standard of living to the highest level in the world!"

The correspondences between this cartoon and Marcos finding Professor Durito while on the run are more than incidental. Again, setting aside the diametrically opposed political ideologies of these two fleeing pairs, the two stories mirror each other. In the cartoon the learners travel to consult a professor in order to untangle the meaning of what they have seen on their tour d'horizon. They're trying to make sense of the orthodoxy of capitalism, which is everywhere, but seeking this consultation puts them right in the sights of a random predator, turning them into refugees in the midst of all of this wealth. In the Zapatista story, the refugee Marcos, who is already fleeing, runs into the professor in the middle of his flight who then turns him into a (reluctant) learner of a new, revolutionary *heterodoxy*.

The main point of commonality between these two pursuit narratives is the oddly out-of-place scene of improvised teaching, which is still somehow connected to being on the run. Both sets of travelers becomes recipients of knowledge, but this happens while they are on the run. And the substance of both teaching scenes is even odder, given the danger from a real pursuing enemy. Both cátedras deal with Big Ideas, with implications that reach well beyond the immediate threat of—respectively—hungry cats and government patrols. But one gets the definite sense that these immediate dangers, and the Big Ideas, are connected.

So what do you do when you are about to be overrun by an overwhelming enemy? From two diametrically opposed political agendas and worldviews comes the same plan. *You stop. To teach. About big things.* And, in the case of the Warner Bros. cartoon (as in most studio cartoons of the period), these pauses make the ultimate outcome possible: unquestionable victory. The "puddytat" (or the coyote, or the tongue-twisted hunter) will always be foiled by the supposedly weaker prey, the urgently needed professor, and the brave resourcefulness this "vulnerable" prey demonstrates in defeating his pursuer extends to the context of his lessons about greater things. The implication is that the broader doctrine of mass production and free markets will ultimately outwit any predator, foreign or domestic, who is trying to eat him and those interested in learning about what he has to say.

Why cartoons to evangelize the Big Ideas? Why resort so often, and at times flippantly, to simple children's allegories or folk tales (like Marcos's 1996 children's book, *The Story of Colors*)? The simple answer is that a time of siege calls for calming and fanciful forms that divert attention *away* from the desperate circumstances—as Chilean writer Ariel Dorfman argued two generations ago in *How to Read Donald Duck: Imperialist Ideology in the Disney Comic* (1971). Consider the triumphalist and euphoric graphics of posters printed during the siege of cities such as Barcelona and Stalingrad: it is only natural to seek solace and shelter in forms that rely on a steadying fantasy world that runs contrary to the desperate realities of the moment—a centrifugal source of psychic energy away from the center of crisis.

But the more credible reason for resorting to simplicity is to tame the enemy by simplifying it. The cartoon cat is an uncomplicated predator who is unsurprisingly defeated by the wily teacher, but during the Cold War the enemy was notoriously wily: abstract and invisible. This speaks to overcoming anxiety in a way that can only exist inside the forced fantasy of a cartoon, which turns the enemy into a quite visible and surmountable cartoon. In the scene with Durito, however, the enemy is no cartoon, and neither are the fleeing soldiers, but Durito, the teacher who is supposed to have all the answers, *is* cartoonish: a curious inversion. Both cases share the representation of a scene of counterfactual conviction: we see believers reaffirming their beliefs, acting on a certainty of what they stand for, despite the odds. For Marcos and his teachers, it is not a question of "if" but "when." Marcos's writings often carry a lyrical tone more fitting to a victorious commander waiting for the surrender of his enemy and considering the humane terms than to a desperate refugee.

A 1995 communiqué features another teacherly interlocutor, the indigenous wise man Old Man Antonio:

> At the committee meeting we discussed throughout the whole afternoon. We searched for the word in [indigenous] language that would mean "surrender" and we could not find one. There is no translation for it, either in Tsotsil or in Tseltal, and no one remembers such a word existing in Tojolabal or Chol. . . . Silently, Antonio comes close to me, coughing with tuberculosis, and whispers in my ear: "That word does not exist in true language, because our people never give up and rather die." (27, my translation)

It is worth noting that the ambitious and totally unrealistic military goal of the Zapatista offensive of January 1, 1994, as announced on Zapatista radio broadcasts, was to "advance to the Capital of the Republic, conquering the Federal Army"—an objective Marcos still insisted upon for several months after the military defeat (Bartolomé 18; Henck 186–68). Of course, triumphalist posturing—characterized by an insistence on the sheer impossibility of failure, an almost irrational conviction of a certain victory—is not unique to Marcos or to the Zapatistas; it is as old as desperate uprisings and resistance movements themselves. The Spanish Civil War motto *no pasarán* ("They shall not pass!") and countless Romantic martyrs ranging from Lord Byron to José Martí and Che Guevara come to mind. But for Marcos and his teacherly alter egos, such as Durito and Old Man Antonio, this response is never jingoistic or shrill, or merely meant to fire up the troops. Instead, the tone is personal and ruminative, and ironic of previous such iterations.

This complicates the one-note sloganeering of the Sandinistas or the Shining Path, and brings to mind the end of Che Guevara's personal *Bolivian Journal*. Just before his capture and death in October 1967, he confides in his diary about a discouraging, growing list of desertions, casualties, material losses, and failures to recruit local support: "It was, without a doubt, the worst month we have had so far" (202). Almost bafflingly, though, he concludes with an optimistic note to himself: "I should mention that Inti and Coco [two of the Cuban guerillas with him] are becoming ever more steadfast revolutionary and military cadres" (202). And then he reports that the "morale of the rest of the men remains fairly high" (220). Is he rallying *himself* with such statements?

When Marcos is recounting his own desperate retreat from the advancing Mexican Army, "Durito asks with pity, as if afraid to hurt me, 'And what do you intend to do?' I keep smoking, I look at the silver curls of the moon hung from the branches. I let out a spiral of smoke and I answer him and myself: 'Win'" (56). The difference between the declarations of faith in an improbable victory in Che's *Journal* and Marcos's output is that Marcos's expression of optimism is *represented:* it is a self-aware act meant for external consumption by a Web-browsing public. This accounts for the common line of descent in these two such dissimilar projects, both in their politics and in their scale—on the one hand the mainstream anticommunist discourse of the Cold War, and on the other the decolonizing discourse of Marcos. Both address the looming Other counterintuitively.

While the Cold War often drove the collective psyche inward—toward comforting, in-charge figures who explain and vanquish the ridiculous enemy (like George Kennan, or the mouse professor who beats the pursuing cat)—Marcos turns this pattern on its head. During the Cold War, one turned to priestly teachers who could explain the big things and calm anxieties, but now, the hieratic teacher to whom one turns is an insufferable and hardly credible little bug. The enemy is quite real and quite dangerous, not a cartoonish cat or an abstract and distant adversary no one will never see, yet the statement by the encircled soldier Marcos, the pupil of this ridiculous new kind of teacher, is eerily familiar: "[I answer] myself: 'Win.'"

Another way to view the recourse to the simplicity of children's narratives is as a deliberate regression, a sort of "strategic infantilization" in the same spirit as literary theorist Gayatri Spivak's notion of "strategic essentialism": a reduction to the "essentials" is necessary for identity politics, made so by the desperate circumstances.[5] This simplifies complex moral problems. Children's allegories, meant to be easily comprehensible, also are comforting when the intended audience is an adult one. And at least in the Disney versions so common in the 1950s, they provided the certainty of the happy ending. Consider the plots of most Disney, MGM, and Warner Bros. cartoons of the 1940s and 1950s: the master narrative is a chase by a larger but ultimately unsuccessful predator. The little mouse will invariably prevail despite the long odds.

These streamlined, escapist narratives comfort children and adults for different reasons. But they act as responses to real anxieties, such as threatening ideologies, fear of the Other, or the actual threat of annihilation. These preoccupations cast their indelible shadows even in the anodyne Disney versions. The very "simplicity" of youth literature, especially cartoons, reveals a complicated relationship to their deadly serious and quite grown-up sources of anxiety, a relationship that cannot be repressed. But the faith in the positive outcome remains strong. It is this memory—of childhood where one could afford to have faith in happy endings—that Marcos knowingly represents, and ironizes, by showing himself as the subject of instruction, not of infantile topics, but by an infantile teacher.

The Intrepid Masked Komrades

We turn briefly to the physical manifestation of Marcos's double voice: his mask. The Zapatista mask is a heavy symbol, much commented on and quite complex. It not only invokes the Mexican Nobel Prize winner Octavio Paz's arguments about the hermetic nature of Mexican character in his essay "Mexican Masks" in 1950's *The Labyrinth of Solitude* (29–46), but also Hollywood fantasies like El Zorro and ninja fighters, and *lucha libre* superheroes and ironizing folk-redeployers such as Mexican urban activist Superbarrio.[6]

An archetypal antihero during the US Cold War, the rebel without a cause, was not "necessarily bad," because, as cultural historians Edward Griffin and Warren Susman argue, he "revolted against a society deserving revolt. Popular writers and professionals had thus arrived at the point where the disturbed personality should be regarded not as a villain but as a hero. Indeed one of the extraordinary features of the period was the celebration of the psychopathic as heroic" (27). An important variant of this antihero, first arising during the 1930s, was the disguised superhero from graphic novels, who fought enemies that tended to be florid, highly stylized evildoers, clear allegories standing in for contemporary threats to the nation: the Depression, gangsterism, fascist totalitarianism, and, finally, communism. These heroes embodied the simple qualities and strengths needed to defeat these allegorical threats; they included, in rough order of appearance, Superman (1938), Batman (1939), Captain America (1941), and Spider-Man (1962).

There is a progression to note in this list. First of all, the transformation of each of these characters into superheroes is increasingly the result of science, technology, and very human knowledge—quite different from the first of them, Superman, with his birthright as a Moses-like prince from outer space. In addition, the nature of the anonymity afforded by the costume changes over time. The "civilian" persona of the superhero started with a bland, civilian incognito (Superman) and went to something more complex. Notice the increasing disconnect between the character's street persona and his crime-fighting, costumed alter ego: when good reporter and good citizen Clark Kent becomes Superman, he casts off his everyman street clothes to become an exaggerated version of his upright-citizen self. He turns into a patriotic showman, garishly heroic in his primary-colored, circus-strongman suit, with bulked-up sense of the same steely civic duty that was already there under his clothes. As Superman, good becomes even more good. His anonymity is not really of much use, because Clark Kent isn't that much different from Superman: a straight talker, honest, helpful, well brought up, out to do good. The difference lies in a pair of eyeglasses and a costume change, and it is a mystery why Lois Lane can't see right through the props. The hero at the end of this list, Spider-Man, is quite different from the virtuous and mostly unconflicted Superman. Peter Parker is an anxious teenager whose superhero persona—the result of a science experiment gone wrong—is an outright fugitive from the law who often uses his powers for dubious ends and is not above vigilantism and revenge. He is conflicted and has many regrets.

This progression from unquestioned hero into edgy quasi-criminal was in part due to the changing nature of the enemy and what was required to defeat it. When the Depression and World War II gave way to the Cold War, the threat to the nation became more ominous, diffuse, and inscrutable. This was no longer a danger that could be tackled by determined patriotic government intervention (in the case of the Depression) or concerted, superior military and industrial might (in the case of the Second World War). The move during the Cold War was toward containment: of the enemy, and of the immediate environment of the ordinary citizenry. And, as we saw in the previous chapter, one response to the enforced domesticity and its stifling closeness was for its rebels to head into the periphery of the wide expanses, into the contrasting enormity of the backcountry, to the open road. But there was another type of reaction for those seeking to confront the enemy head on: to become, albeit increasingly conflicted, masked do-gooders.

Marcos is a late redeployment of this Cold War cultural pattern, now fueled by a keen irony and a sense of self-awareness. In the original Cold War dynamic of the 1950s in the United States, the enemy was perpetually imminent, as well as immanent: always about to strike, always nowhere and everywhere at once. This duality undergirds the superheroes' anonymity/public persona of the period, projecting an external paradox into an internal conflict between the two sides of the same character: the private "civilian" and public crime-fighting "superhero," a dichotomy that only increased over time.[7]

The public crime fighters Batman and Spider-Man were progressively shadier, to the point of quasi-criminality, in contrast with their upstanding-citizen cover personas, which remained stable. Batman began as a violent, gray-area extension of hard-boiled fiction and gradually became even darker and subject to questionable motivations for his violence. From the beginning Spider-Man operated as an outright vigilante outside the rule of law. The sideshow masks joined to the alter-ego "normal" existences become more and more a necessary prerequisite for doing "good," precisely because this dualism allowed superheroes to operate outside the rule of law. These heroes' bland, anonymized cover personas contrasted more and more with their dark work as bringers of irregular justice.[8] The chronological list of masked superheroes, each more marginal and more conflicted, reaches a turning point—an ironic, self-aware turnabout—in its postmodern postscript: Marcos.

In a dispatch from January 20, 1994, Marcos offers this taunt: "Why so much ruckus about the ski-masks? Isn't Mexican political culture of 'culture of hidden faces'? But in order to put a stop to the anguish of those who are afraid (or who wish) that some 'Komrade' or cartoon villain might be the one who would appear behind the ski mask, . . . of the 'Sup'. . . . I propose the following: I am willing to take off my mask if Mexican Society takes off its foreign mask that it anxiously put on years ago" (Marcos et al. 86). Besides the somewhat predictable challenge to society—that he will drop the pretense of the mask if society does the same thing—he warns that what is underneath the mask might be quite frightening: a cartoon character, a communist "Komrade."

Marcos's masked strategy interlaces with another familiar Cold War figure: the knowing professor. All the oracles from Kennan onward had worked to unmask the enemy as large and unthinking. But, alternatively, Marcos's masked professor is almost *too* knowing; he knows more about the enemy than the enemy knows about itself. Marcos's disguises and anonymity recall Churchill's speech in academic drag, a professorial garb not really his own, as well as Kennan's "Long Telegram." But his outsider condition, although fully expected for a superhero, is no longer a representation of an inability to fit into the world at large. Instead, the criminality *reflects* the outside world: Mexican officialdom is the real criminal here. Marcos's "anonymity" is a fake, an effigy to call attention to bigger fakes.

This returns us to the initial contradiction of Marcos's discourse, one that was also central to the Cold War condition: the simultaneous coexistence of two scales, one small and one large. On the one hand is the pragmatic struggle for indigenous rights, and on the other the much larger war against enormous (and slippery) world-scale threats such as "neoliberalism" and "globalization." Nuancing this dichotomy, Kristine Vanden Berghe argues that there is an intermediate third scale in Marcos's discourse—a national one. She contends that Marcos's Zapatismo was essentially an attempt to reclaim the national register, "discredit the government," and "dissociate it from Mexico, its geography, its history, and the aspirations of its people" (Vanden Berghe 134, my translation; Vanden Berghe and Maddens 125). This reading would locate 1990s Zapatista discourse within a long continuum of patriotic nationalism, more specifically the effort to claim the "authentic" legacy of the Mexican Revolution of 1910. This is quite visible in the EZLN's and Marcos's transformation from the FLN "Frente de Liberación Nacional" (National Liberation Front) into the "Ejército Zapatista de Liberación Nacional" (Zapatista Army of National Liberation)—or, as Nick Henck details, from a "People's Guerilla" to a "Guerilla people" (64–190).

Some analysts have taken this further to argue that the EZLN was a neonationalist organization. In any case, it points to an important aspect of Zapatismo necessary to understand its central paradox: its place, its "geography." One key geography of the Cold War was an internal, infinitely repeated small space: the domestic. It was seen in the glow of TV sets, in countless living rooms where it played out. This seemingly calm domesticity spoke to the enormous mental fortitude that was required; it provided constancy and predictability. These stories of professors on the run—the Durito stories and the "Mouse" cartoon—share an important departure from this idealized domestic location of safety. The reassuring acts of teaching occur wherever one is momentarily safe from a circling enemy. They happen on the road. Again, "cátedra" refers to both the content of a lecture (the message) and its location (the chair). The places of these lectures on the run are always improvised, anything but routine.

Not all improvisations are equal. Durito from his cátedra explains how the enemy's failing is its way of improvising: the neoliberal government hunting them down will ultimately fail because it operates by "i-m-p-r-o-v-i-s-a-t-i-o-n. The government has no consistency" and "no plans . . . no perspectives," he states—from his own oddly *improvised* yet almost complete classroom. The government has a different kind of improvisation than his, an unthinking and (literally) reactionary one. Durito's brand of improvisation is different: it is one of resourcefulness, of resilience, and smallness—a perspective lacking in the pursuing federal forces. By pulling out the accoutrements of the classroom in the middle of the jungle, flip chart and desk included, he establishes the connection between the rebellion's local struggle and a much larger one that affects everyone. He is following Che Guevara's famous dictum about improvising the revolution: "It is not necessary to wait until all conditions for making revolution exist; the insurrection can create them." A little one-desk classroom in the jungle, while one is on the run, can have a significant impact—especially when it broadcasts over the Web (7).

Size matters. Especially if you're a small cartoonish creature, most threats will always appear oversized; in later communiqués, Durito mounts an "anti-boot" campaign. But one's smallness also confers a visionary privilege, because the scale and perspective of the enterprise is inverted. The specific threats in the local conflicts sublimate into a larger ideological message on a grander scale. But a small creature cannot forget smallness. The colonialism scholars Jean and John Comaroff, echoing Hardt and Negri, have observed that, in the class struggle at the millennium, the strategy of the ruling class—globalizing neoliberalism—has involved outsourcing labor into the realm of the virtual by dissipating its specific locations. Globalization is "likely to fragment modernist forms of class consciousness, class alliance and class antinomies. . . .It is also likely to dissolve the ground on which proletarian culture once took shape" (302). In a fundamental way, smallness of scale stands in opposition to such deterritorialization. Smallness by necessity is closer to its very physical immediacy.

The Zapatista slogan of the *first* Zapata, during the Revolution of 1910–20, was one of place, of land reform: "The land belongs to those who work it" (*la tierra es de quien la trabaja*). This *cri* becomes more complicated when the land that is in contention is virtual, existing in cyberspace. It holds to reason that the local struggle would be undermined by the virtualization of one of the tools of resistance, the *cátedra*, into the more diffuse but farther-reaching scale of the Web. But, in important ways, this can be read as a way to reclaim the means of production, the virtual locality: fighting fire with fire, taking the battle to the ether, turning virtual space into the local because that is where injustice is now effected.

The unprecedented battle of the EZLN and (Neo)Zapatismo for digital land reform channels the original Zapatismo's specific goals. This brings us once more to Marcos's double discourse, and to his knowing deployment of the conventions and strategies of the Cold War. In a communiqué from September 4, 1995, Durito himself takes up the keyboard and invents for himself a persona as a Quixotic "Don Durito de la Lacandona," with the *Sup* Marcos as his squire. He issues the following slapstick parable. (I include the Spanish original to highlight an untranslatable linguistic particularity, the comic abuse of diminutive endings for the nouns ["-ito, -ita"].)

> Once upon a time there was a little mouse who was very hungry. He wanted to eat a little bit of cheese that was in the little kitchen of a little house. So the little mouse very sure of himself headed for the little kitchen to take the little bit of cheese. But it so happens that a little kitty came across his way. . . . So then the little mouse said,
>
> "Enough already!" and he grabbed a machine gun and riddled the little kitty and then went into the kitchen and saw that the little bit of fish, the bit of milk and the bit of cheese had gone bad and were inedible. So he went back to where the cat was, and he dismembered him and then made a great roast and then he invited all his little friends and they had a party and they ate the roasted kitty and they sang and danced and lived happily ever after.
>
> (Ejército Zapatista de Liberación Nacional, Mexico, 438–39, my translation)

> (Había una vez un ratoncito que tenía mucha hambre y quería comer un quesito que estaba en la cocinita de la casita. Y entonces el ratoncito se fue muy decidido a la cocinita para agarrar el quesito, pero resulta que se le atravesó un gatito. . . . Y entonces el ratoncito dijo:
>
> —"¡Ya basta!"—y agarró una ametralladora y acribilló al gatito y fue a la cocinita y vio que el pescadito, la lechita y el quesito ya se habían echado a perder y ya no se podían comer y entonces regresó a donde estaba el gatito y lo destazó y luego hizo un gran asado y luego invitó a todos sus amiguitos y amiguitas y entonces hicieron una fiesta y se comieron al gatito asado y cantaron y bailaron y vivieron muy felices.)

Diminutives turn things small. Here the overuse is a parody of the treacly tone of stories for young children, where the diminutives create a sense of innocence and intimacy. In this case it contrasts sharply with the ultraviolent ending, making it even more jarring. (Durito, the little hard one, is no soft touch.) Irony is related to scale.

The small-scale, local goal of the original (Neo)Zapatismo was attainment of indigenous rights in the state of Chiapas. This required unironic and straightforward language and a clearly defined outcome, echoing the language of similar revolutions. It is to the point. During this first phase of the campaign, Marcos was willing and capable of marshaling such language. The early *declaraciones* still have faith in instruments such as the Mexican Constitution, which unequivocally states that the people have the absolute right to change the government if it no longer reflects the will of the people. It is a sincere and heartfelt belief in the social contract. A hopeful communiqué from August 30, 1995, during peace talks with the government (only a few days before Durito's ironic parable), proclaims that "effort by Mexicans, citizens, and the National Peace Conference reminds us that the motherland [*patria*] lives and is ours" (Ejército Zapatista de Liberación Nacional 437, my translation). This may sound naïve, but it is issued in the good faith that the government could still abide by its own values in making decisions about this local struggle. It is meant for internal consumption. In contrast, just a few days later when Marcos launches into the larger-scale dimension of Zapatismo, into the struggle against globalization and neoliberalism, his message is voiced ironically (and certainly more entertainingly) by a "tiny" voice: the diminutive and pompous Durito. It is meant to project to an outside audience; his smallness helps.

Understandably, most interpreters are more drawn to the "postmodern" Marcos—ironic, complicated, and self-referential, a masked figure who speaks to the world in savvy terms—than to the idealistic Marcos, who voices worry about the daily caloric intake of the indigenous Tzotzil population. This playful, ironic Marcos is as much a performer as a revolutionary; he fits into a long tradition of countercultural activity mixing art and activism ("culture jamming," or, more recently, "artivism"), with deep roots in Dada, Surrealism, French Situationism, and other avant-gardes. This tradition is part aesthetic gesture, part grand political statement, and part juvenile pranksterism, but mostly performance.[9] Marcos as ethereal commentator and social and intellectual gadfly is more persistent than the guns-and-bullets guerilla leader actively fighting for local change: he is more valuable as a revolutionary critic than as an actual revolutionary.[10] The progression of the Marcos persona might warrant the claim that he himself orchestrated that transformation. After the stalemate of 1994–96, when the real-world, geographic impact of the EZLN vanished, and violent conflict segued into seemingly endless negotiation, the only viable Marcos was really the virtual Marcos of indefinite time and space, long-term goals, and rhetorical mastery. The actual physical battle was over.

Finally, recall an important fact about the ironic Marcos of this countercultural tradition, master of a sophisticated and antiglobalizing wit, who aims to decolonize the patterns of the Cold War discourse. That ironic and slippery Marcos, at least for a time, coexisted in equal measure with the "real" Marcos, who was hiding in the sierra with an underequipped force, issuing sincere demands and engaging in real violence. The grounded Marcos still had in mind a solution (if small-scale), echoing previous, dead-serious voices like Fidel Castro's in the "Declaraciones de la Habana." And these two coexisting modes, one adamant and the other wistful, were on a fundamental level still hoping for a home, something that the more gestural revolutionaries like the cosmopolitan Situationists could take for granted. Home, a plot of land to call their own, was something that neither Marcos nor Zapatismo could ever take for granted. Although Marcos's ironic redeployment of Cold War discourse shares much with the Situationists, it is fundamentally different, because it does not happen in the metropolis—in Paris or New York or even Mexico City—at the heart of empire, in any hegemonic center of geography. It is, and always will be, located in the backwoods periphery, which is now in cyberspace. And because of this its reach has been enormous.

5 Doesn't He Ever Learn?
Denis Johnson's *Jesus' Son* and the Weight of Knowledge, or a Second Chance for a Lonely Picaro

No one can see for those who don't see, or turn another's ignorance into knowledge. The problem is not about knowing what you are doing. That kind of knowledge, despite what the clever say, is the most commonly widespread. The problem is to think about what you are doing, to remember yourself.
—Jacques Rancière, "Un enfant se tue" (my translation)

I hurt myself today
To see if I still feel
—Nine Inch Nails, "Hurt"

WE COME to the late twentieth century, during the end stages of empire, when one of the downsides of trying to find someplace to get away to is that there is nowhere left to run. Everything is there, perhaps decrepit, but visible.

This study began by distinguishing between two kinds of travel narratives: those about the individual traveler, and those about the traveling pair. I have suggested many parallels between their respective histories and their related literary genres and argued for the association of the first with the picaresque and the second with the quixotic. This study's gathering of texts was organized to point to a progression, reflecting the relationship between two forms of identity, the individual and the national. And, in the process of exploring this relationship, I invoked such enormous, interrelated concepts as exceptionalism, Latin American *americanismo*, and what I call "empire without empire." The basic assumption was a seamless link between sociohistorical forces and cultural production.

I am not alone in linking *longue durée* patterns of collective identity and history to the evolution of aesthetic forms. But it is daunting to acknowledge that this line of argument has led some great pessimists to conclude, more often than not, that there is a decline, some sort of waning of history, mirrored in the slow decay of a once-dominant aesthetic form (or vice versa).

The Marxist literary critic György Lukács theorized decline by maintaining that when modernity and its mercantilist bourgeois values clashed against the grand form of the epic, the ultimate outcome was a lesser genre, the novel—inferior, in his view, to the previous, grand narrative form. On the other end of the political register and following the lead of Oswald Spengler's *The Decline of the West* (1918) are literary critics such as Northrop Frye, who argued for archetypal cycles of history and aesthetics, and Harold Bloom, whose work is obsessed with belatedness and the idea of knowledge arriving to seekers too late to be of any good. Both of these critics work in a plaintive, conservative voice, driven by a sense that things will soon fall apart, that centers will not hold. In their view, the bellwether aesthetic forms and sensibilities sometimes offer a last refuge—a defense against that coming deterioration—and perhaps leave hints of things as they once were, before the decadence and decline. Future, enlightened readers, it is implied, *may* find hope in this.

End-stage aesthetics usually involves a keen sense of self-awareness, of knowing precisely where and what is being lost. The Baroque consciously and meticulously reread an exhausted mannerism; modernism fastidiously considered and rejected an exhausted Romanticism; postmodernism deconstructed modernism. And these "post" periods often produced a tone, a sensibility of elegiac self-awareness. Late reflective turns that bemoan lost beginnings are often reifications in the Marxist sense: they can't avoid repeating, rematerializing the previous form and sensibility, which happens to be exhausted or moribund.

This is why so many "late" styles are urbane and ironic, as Frye would have it, generating what he has called the "winter" mode. Sometimes this late style offers a celebration of that something that's gone, even if it's gone for good reason. And sometimes it is a simple but knowing reflection of things that have become too familiar, as when American writer John Barth argued in 1967 that postmodernism was a "literature of exhaustion."[1]

For our purposes it would be tempting to stress the notion that, in recent decades, the end of empire in America (the United States) is so prevalent that it is ingrained in the nation's cultural production—including its travel literature—but I won't venture quite that far. I will, however, break my pattern of looking at pairs of travelers of empire and conclude this study by considering the story of a single traveler going through a very rough journey for and by himself, one that resonates in a knowing, self-reflective way with all the patterns I've suggested in the preceding pages, including patterns of empire. And the setting of the last work I consider here, Denis Johnson's novel *Jesus' Son* (1993), takes place when the twilight of empire announces itself in a million ways.

Jesus' Son, craftily adapted to a film of the same name by director Alison Maclean (1999), is composed of a series of linked vignettes set in the Midwest and the West during the early 1970s. The narrator and protagonist, known only as "Fuckhead" (an epithet slapped on him by a rival), is a young wanderer and drug addict who seems never to have held a steady job. In good picaresque form he moves episodically through several dubious "apprenticeships." He works as a hospital assistant, where another orderly teaches him how to steal prescriptions from the lockup. He becomes a rural drug dealer supplying various flophouses. He learns from an acquaintance how to steal copper wiring from a construction site. After one hard day of laboring at this last activity, he admits to the unfamiliar but satisfying "feeling of men who had worked" (66).

In classic picaro form, the narrator's amoral survival instinct helps him bear the inevitable hard knocks of life, which he recounts in a deadpan first person, full of passivity, and to painfully comic effect. After accompanying a girlfriend to get an illegal abortion, the pair holes up in a motel, but then she runs off with another man and dies of an overdose. He tells this horrific sequence of events mutedly, in a passionless voice, with a childlike wonder that is both hilarious and disturbing.

Immunity to pain is an insistent pattern with Fuckhead as well as many others in his drug-addled world, but he often wonders aloud about that immunity. It seems to surprise him still. When he goes looking for someone named McInnes at a drug house, he stumbles onto his friend Dundun casually pumping water in the yard. Dundun informs him that "McInnes isn't feeling too good today. I just shot him" (45). Fuckhead goes into the house and indeed finds this to be the case. McInness is slowly dying on the sofa, and no one seems to care very much—as if he were just one more incapacitated junkie. But Fuckhead offers to take him to the emergency room. In another scene, when Fuckhead is working as a hospital orderly, a man walks into the hospital complaining about a headache—because he has a hunting knife sticking out of his eye socket. While the alarmed hospital staff goes into high gear, setting up for a major trauma intervention, when nobody is looking Fuckhead simply pulls out the offending knife with a clean jerk, solving the problem.

His own immunity to pain does not translate into a callous heartlessness; often he ends up doing the right thing in many bad situations, often in spite of himself. But even if he is not always aware of the implications of the scenes before him, he is quite aware of his own numbness to pain and tragedy. The story of his wanderings can be read as a search for a way to puncture this utter lack of feeling, to experience something that he can sense "for real" and possibly end the seemingly endless, horrific scenes in which he appears to be stuck—and stuck not really caring about them, though he often goes through the motions trying to make things better.

In one early episode he lands in a hospital after a road accident. In his mind this occasion starts blending with another time when he found himself in a clinical setting, at a detox center in Seattle:

> "Are you hearing unusual sounds or voices?" the doctor asked.
> "Help us, oh God, it hurts," the boxes of cotton screamed.
> "Not exactly," I said. . . .
> "How did the room get so white?" I asked. A beautiful nurse was touching my skin. "These are vitamins," she said, and drove a needle in. It was raining. Gigantic ferns leaned over us. The forest drifted down a hill. I could hear a creek rushing down among the rocks. And you, you ridiculous people, you expect me to help you. (12)

The cartoonish boxes of cotton are the ones in physical pain, not him: he can only watch as they scream. The needle jabbing into his own arm barely registers. The mock put-down of his readers as "ridiculous" is because they might expect him to care, might require him to "help"—to feel something for them, which he just can't seem to manage at this particular moment.

The formal elements of the "original" picaresque as inaugurated by the *Lazarillo de Tormes* in the sixteenth century, are all hyperevident in Johnson's novel: in the episodic architecture of delinquent apprenticeships, for instance, in the confessional first person, the overarching nihilism, and the imperative to keep moving. But it is also possible to see this text as a descendant of a later kind of picaresque, the eighteenth-century version, of clueless optimists like Rasselas or Candide. Fuckhead's curiously optimistic view of reality is just as dubious as theirs, and as a result the satire is quite intense. Fuckhead wanders through a world that is much nastier and more aggressive than he could ever be, so that world is hardly ever under his control. But, unlike his somewhat wooden and two-dimensional predecessors—those eighteenth-century picaros whose stupidity translates into satirical resilience—modernity treats Fuckhead differently. He is a fairly realistic creature, in that sense perhaps truer to the original picaresque. He is credible as a *representation* of a lost, drugged-out wanderer whose naïveté and optimism are merely symptoms. His claims of clairvoyance and irrational exuberance seem to credible attributes of someone caught in a chemically induced reality, so the question of the narrator's perception of the world and the associated truth claims once again comes to the forefront.

To reprise the distinction between the lonely picaro and the pairs of travelers considered in the previous chapters, the main difference lies in a pair's (in)capacity to perceive the world, and themselves, because of their complicated involvement with each other—critic Leelah Gandhi's "catoptrics." As she says, "No catoptrics can mirror back to them, these shallowest, most surface-bound beings, the historical disaster that they portend" (18). Traveling pairs just don't "get it." There is so much they just can't see. But the possibility of deep perception, and even of addressing perception itself, comes to *Jesus' Son* with a vengeance. This wandering picaro, in his drug-addled state of heightened awareness, is obsessed with his own process of awareness.

At the outset of the book there is a terrible car accident. Fuckhead had been hitchhiking in search of his missing girlfriend. He's already hitched a number of rides in the rain, from various drivers:

> A salesman who shared his liquor and steered while sleeping . . . A Cherokee filled with bourbon . . . A VW no more than a bubble of hashish fumes, captained by a college student . . . And a family from Marshalltown who head-onned and killed forever a man driving west out of Bethany, Missouri. . . . My jaw ached. I knew every raindrop by its name. I sensed everything before it happened. I knew a certain Oldsmobile would stop for me even before it slowed, and by the sweet voices of the family inside it I knew we'd have an accident in the storm. I didn't care. They said they'd take me all the way. The man and the wife put the little girl up front with them and left the baby in the back with me and my dripping bedroll. (3–4)

Fuckhead survives this horrific crash and flags down a passing trailer truck for help. Everyone is taken to the hospital, where he witnesses the following scene:

> Down the hall came the wife. She was glorious, burning. She didn't know yet that her husband was dead. We knew. That's what gave her such power over us. The doctor took her into a room with a desk at the end of the hall, and from under the closed door a slab of brilliance radiated as if, by some stupendous process, diamonds were being incinerated in there. What a pair of lungs! She shrieked as I imagined an eagle would shriek. I felt wonderful to be alive to hear it! I've gone looking for that feeling everywhere. (11)

In a still from the film (see fig. 8), the camera witnesses the scene from the point of view of the narrator, who is watching the unfolding agony of the just-informed wife. The framing is quite telling. The hyperbolically bright square of the window intensifies the contrast between the viewer, who is outside the frame in relative darkness, and the intensely emotional and well-lit place of the revelation happening in the room. The distance between the wife in pain and the viewers is heightened even more by the sound: her muted screams are barely audible behind the glass. Like Velázquez's 1656 painting *Las meninas,* the exaggerated chiaroscuro framing intensifies the distance between us as viewers and the drama in front of us. The viewer becomes part of the distancing, aestheticizing artifice.

This chiaroscuro also highlights a temporal contrast between the two kinds of awareness at play here, two altered—exalted—mental states. The drugged-out, hyperaware narrator and the newly widowed woman inhabit their respective knowledge(s) in very different ways. Whereas Fuckhead's awareness is a constant and inescapable weight on him (he has "always known" of his own omniscience, perhaps a product of his chemical dependence), the widow's knowledge is sudden, it is *now*. It hits her all at once, this moment of tragedy, in a blinding flash with a clear "before" and "after." For this witnessing picaro, awareness works quite the opposite; he already knows and sees, too much to experience something as emotional, as blindingly bright, as the "glorious, burning" pain of the widow.

Recall a fundamental insistence of the original picaresque, the imperative to be an eyewitness to "truth." This imperative is put to the test radically in this example of late picaresque. Fuckhead's claims of witnessing reliably stretch into the irrational: he claims, God-like, to be able to see and know just about everything about a particular moment—its before and after—far exceeding the typical truth claim of the typical picaresque survivor. Fuckhead claims vision that reaches the point of omniscience, a kind of atemporality, of being beyond the confines of time ("I sensed everything before it happened. I knew a certain Oldsmobile would stop for me even before it slowed").

Fuckhead's powerful and all-knowing awareness greatly magnifies a weight familiar to the original picaro: the deep, ontological sense of loneliness. It is more palpable here than in many of the countless picaresques that came before. His omniscience made him despondently "always know" that he was destined to play a part in that night's horrific drama, and this inescapable awareness makes him "not care." Inevitability, the foreknowledge of things to come, compounds the sense of being terribly alone even further. Because he can't be surprised by it, Fuckhead is unaffected by the tragedy's shock value. He is, however, also aware of his own self-detachment, and he often reaches in vain for something, someone, beyond himself in order to ground himself again. In the scene at the hospital, his omniscient "I" expands to become "*we* knew," revealing a yearning to belong to a community of like feeling, to others like him who are numb. It is not clear to whom the "we" refers—perhaps the medical staff standing around him—but he clearly wants a collective "I" to witness and share along with him the young woman's pain.

Like the optimistic eighteenth-century picaros of chapter 2, Fuckhead's numerous tragedies—and even the cognitive weight of their inevitability—do not drive him to either desperation or cynicism. He keeps moving, even happily. He is stoically and comically blunt ("She shrieked as I imagined an eagle would shriek. I felt wonderful to be alive to hear it!"), but somehow above the fray despite the very real loss and dislocation going on in front of him. He remains a desperate optimist, if a deeply lonely one. Even bearing the weight of such knowledge, an awareness of all the bad things that can and will happen to him and to others around him, he manages to retain a sense of wonder. His curiosity is not about what the future can hold—he already knows that, being fully aware of the misfortunes in store for him. Instead, his fascination is about other people: those who still *don't* know their fate, the mere mortals who, like this newly widowed woman and unlike him, can still suffer the shock of the unexpected.

His curiosity, his yearning, is reserved for the only thing he *can't* know: what it would be like to be someone *who doesn't know everything*. He can only imagine that. He longs for the mind of someone who hasn't yet been sullied and weighted down by the hyperknowledge that shackles him, yearns for a prelapsarian condition: "I've gone looking for that feeling everywhere" (11). He hungers for the innocence of the widow just before she knows she has become a widow. He envies her at that precise moment when innocence ends and she falls into knowledge, horrific or not—the instant she reaches awareness.

Essentially he suffers from trauma envy.

Witnessing the tragic transformation of the young woman is "wonderful" to him and gives him a "feeling of life unlike any other"; he has "gone looking for that feeling everywhere." It gives him a vicarious, drug-like rush and propels him into a lifetime of seeking it out. His real compulsion, his true addiction, is to a state of innocence.

Omniscience for this picaro doesn't translate into omnipotence—quite the contrary. For Fuckhead his awareness is a paralyzing burden, much like drug addiction itself. This fallen wanderer knows so much that he's far beyond the kind of cluelessness—philosopher Avital Ronell's "stupidity," discussed in chapter 1—that paradoxically can lead to true insight. Instead of possessing the kind of ignorance with which the stupid somehow hold power over knowledge (even if they don't *get* it), his excess of knowledge holds power over *him*.

Voyeur, Voyager

> It has been said that the pervert does not do drugs. Perhaps this refers to actions that are executed with guiltless precision.
> —Avital Ronell, *Crack Wars*

> Because if I'd a knowed what a trouble it was to make a book I wouldn't a tackled it, and ain't a-going to no more. But I reckon I got to light out for the Territory ahead of the rest, because Aunt Sally she's going to adopt me and sivilize me, and I can't stand it. I been there before.
> THE END. YOURS TRULY, *HUCK FINN*.
> —Mark Twain, *The Adventures of Huckleberry Finn*

The title of Johnson's novel comes from Lou Reed's Velvet Underground song "Heroin" (1967):

> I don't know just where I'm going
> But I'm gonna try for the kingdom, if I can
> 'Cause it makes me feel like I'm a man
> When I put a spike into my vein
> And I tell you things aren't quite the same
> When I'm rushing on my run
> And I feel just like Jesus' son
> And I guess that I just don't know
> And I guess that I just don't know

These stanzas point to a triad of contrasting impulses that resolve in a sonnet-like progression. First is a grandiose and futile attempt at totality, at going for the brass ring—"gonna try for the Kingdom." Second is a gesture of self-correction, when the speaker recognizes his limitations—he is stuck, in this case by addiction—which in turn makes him feel caught in a paradox, like being the nonexistent "son" of Jesus (or perhaps in the paralyzing role having an impossible act to follow). And third is a repetition of "I just don't know," driving home the acknowledgement of the existential doubt, the result of being trapped in a quandary. Likewise, although the narrator of *Jesus' Son* has suffered plenty of traumas, none has yet developed to the point of healing, of transcendence. He is stuck in a post-trauma without the possibility of overcoming it. He can't unsee or unlearn, but he can't yet feel, either.

He hopes that by witnessing and inhabiting *someone else*'s experience, someone else's trauma he can borrow that someone's "abreaction"—the therapeutic release that comes from having survived and thus getting a chance to address, and overcome, the effects of trauma. He longs to transform himself vicariously in order to start feeling again. He's operating under the premise that he can return to the ranks of those who feel and thus reexperience the deep rush of life. He hopes that by getting close to a stranger's defining first trauma, he can borrow it as if it were his own. His only hope for a cure for his affective indifference—for knowing too much—is returning to the "just don't know" state: a vulnerable, unstable condition that will let him experience the other's pain, and perhaps understand and overcome it, and by extension his own. But this is not to be. He is too numb, he knows too much. When he hears about his girlfriend's death by overdose, even this close-to-home tragedy doesn't generate any significant effect in him.

So can this picaro unlearn? Can he recover? In the book's final vignette, we find Fuckhead living in Phoenix, finally kicking the drugs, participating in a step program, and finding himself "in a little better physical shape every day." He has discovered a routine and has finally stopped traveling. Phoenix: a city whose name speaks to rising from the ashes and to second chances. He is working part time at a home for mentally and physically handicapped old people. He blurts out about himself: "I was getting my looks back, and my spirits were rising.... All these weirdos, and me getting better every day right in the midst of them. I had never known, never imagined for a heartbeat, that there might be a place for us" (160). On his daily walk to work he spies through a bathroom window on a young woman taking a shower and singing. He makes it part of his routine to walk by at the same time of day in order to see her. He notes that she wears long skirts and that the husband has an "Abraham Lincoln beard"—so he surmises that they might be "Amish or more likely Mennonites": "Stopping there and watching while she showered, watching her step out naked, dry off, and leave the bathroom, and then listening to the sounds her husband made coming home in his car and walking through the front door, all of this became part of my routine. . . . I didn't learn any of her secrets, though I wanted to, especially because she didn't know me. She probably couldn't have even imagined me" (147). This is an appropriate conclusion to a picaresque journey of a late-stage picaro who has reached self-awareness: the picaro as voyeur. His travels, and his search to inhabit other people's trauma, have finally ended. The picaro's wandering education, usually a sequence of failures, has progressed to the point of settlement.

The typical picaresque tour d'horizon of a semisettled and harsh world is part of an ultimate plea for lenience, an excuse for his bad choices. But the tour of the underworld is reduced to a tour of the body of an innocent Mennonite woman, without her knowledge or consent. Unlike the new widow after the car crash, screaming because her innocence is forever transformed by her husband's death, this showering woman gets to keep her innocence. Fuckhead is content being a trespassing witness to her everyday routine from within his own numb and mundane routine: he is at peace with the knowledge that this woman's psyche is so different from his that she couldn't have "even imagined him." He is reaching, not for her awareness, but for her ignorance: to be unimagined by her. She, as the Lou Reed song says, "just doesn't know" him.

The first woman he spied on through a window, the new widow at the beginning of his travels (see fig. 8) was remarkable to him because she was someone at the precise moment of losing her innocence, of falling into knowledge due to a horrible event. But this Mennonite woman will remain safe: she will never know him, and if he stays safely in the shrubbery she will completely avoid the trauma of the personal violation being committed upon her. And he is part of that continuing ignorance.

He's watching, for certain, but now from within the limits of his own vision and his own experience. He is no longer omniscient; he does not wish to be part of her trauma in order to take it from her any longer. This is a workable arrangement, one of mutual nonknowledge, since she can't "even imagine him," and all he will know of her will be her routine, her nakedness, but no other details. He will remain unknown to her, sparing her a devastating invasion and the inevitable transformation that revelation would wreak upon her. He is a secret voyeur, not a predator or a transgressor.

In his seminal work on blindness and insight, the critic Paul de Man elaborates on the sense of effortlessness that can happen when one becomes comfortable with intricate, preestablished patterns (de Man writes of dancing masters, marionettes, and sword fencing). But if one

Figure 8. "What a pair of lungs!" Still from *Jesus' Son,* directed by Alison Maclean (2:54)

suddenly starts thinking about the patterns, this self-awareness can lead to sudden clumsiness, or even paralysis. De Man inserts an oddly personal anecdote. He recalls having read in the newspaper that when one drives a car, thirty-six conscious decisions happen for every hundred meters of driving. After reading this, he reports, he was no longer able to drive. His sense of temporality—of what happens within a very specific given period of time—was ruined (Rhetoric 277). For most of *Jesus' Son,* the narrator has been free of any progressive sense of temporality: his perception of time is total: nonsequential, and all-encompassing. But at the end of his travels and now in recovery, he has become established in the rather routine present—a job, a schedule, a twelve-step program, a regular peek through a window. He is now firmly within a fairly pedestrian routine, a linear chronology.

One of the more astute critics of the traumatic model of cognition, Lauren Berlant, writes that, given the end of the likelihood of conventional global war in the Cold War and post–Cold War periods, the late-capitalist "present" has heavily diminished the possibility of collective trauma. The "good life" has become a convenient and pervasive fiction, and using and expecting traumatic knowledge is no longer possible, replaced by the prospect of total annihilation. Instead, the drab, relatively affluent present belongs to what she calls "crisis ordinariness" (81). In *Jesus' Son,* Fuckhead's job in the group home is to run the daily newsletter. He fills it with ordinariness: with cheery birthday reminders, menus, bland health advice, chatty nothings. He likes this mundane ephemerality. Like the main character Murdock in Jorge Luis Borges's story "The Ethnographer" discussed in the opening chapter, Fuckhead has become settled, even banal, after his life-changing experiences (Borges, *Fictions* 335). Now he writes tame reports for a sedated audience, rather than telling stories from the dark underside where he used to lurk. In this late-stage picaresque, the challenge of venturing out to the backcountry to "see what is out there" and even seeing "what is *in* there"—in his own unsettled psyche—has been exhausted. It has become simple, made corporeal. Like many of the Enlightenment picaros before him, Fuckhead had been wandering in avoidance of bourgeois respectability, resisting the pull of Robinson Crusoe's "middle station," but now, like Crusoe, he has finally arrived there.

He has also finally learned that regaining innocence is an impossible goal, so his settling down is a fully self-aware reentry into the stasis of life's middle station: a job, sobriety, a sense of getting somewhere by being consistently somewhere, rather than by endless wandering. But this stage of self-awareness has come at a high cost. He has had to give up hope of ever reclaiming the prelapsarian existence, and *that* knowledge weighs on him ("you, you ridiculous people, you expect me to help you"). This forfeiture of his initial object of his impossible desire—innocence—strengthens his sense of affinity with the broken and dying people of the halfway house. These people, "freaks" like him, have suffered a cosmic injustice that makes "God look like a senseless maniac."

God is dead, or at least reduced to a senseless maniac. But Fuckhead now has found a place for star-crossed "weirdos" like him who have suffered from God's misbehavior. His own handicap is that he has seen too much, knows too much, like Nietzsche's "overman." The overman is that rare individual who has become painfully aware that life is an inescapable set of cycles (the "eternal return"), and one of the even fewer with the superhuman energy to withstand the weight of that knowledge without going mad. The strong are those who are too heavily weighed down, who bear inescapable burdens, but who do as Ennis del Mar says in "Brokeback Mountain": "If you can't fix it you've got to stand it" (269). And Fuckhead is now okay with that burden.

Notes

To the Reader

1. See Lewis Hanke and Gustavo Pérez Firmat. A comprehensive state-of-the art survey of the field has been recently offered by Earl E. Fitz.

Introduction

1. The nomenclature of the region is politically charged. I use the terms historically, referring to the region as "Spanish America" before independence and "Latin America" after that, or (as in this case) when referring to its entire history.

2. It is useful to recognize the vast and significant body of work on pastoralism and on the epistemological distinction between city and the country, most notably along the Marxist lines of the theorist Raymond Williams in *The Country and the City* (1973).

3. Indian raids and the threat of Indian captivity are a fixture of frontier culture of the United States, and there are also notable Latin American examples—for instance, from the South American pampas is *La cautiva (The captive,* 1837) by the Argentinian Romantic writer Esteban Echevarría. On female Indian captivity, see two parallel studies, Christopher Castiglia's *Bound and Determined,* for the North American phenomenon, and Susana Rotker's *Captive Women,* for the South American one. When the US government began persecuting the Comanche, Kiowa, and Apache, many of these tribes retreated into northern Mexico, especially in the 1840s and 1850s, causing an escalation of raids within Mexico that even threatened Mexico City (Weber 95). In his memoirs recalling childhood on the northern deserts during the 1890s, the Mexican politician and philosopher José Vasconcelos, author of the influential *The Cosmic Race* (1926), recalls being warned by his mother what would happen to him if he were captured by marauding Indians (1:7–8).

4. My translation of "¿Buscaremos la higiene y patología del hombre chileno en los libros europeos, y no estudiaremos hasta qué punto es modificada la organización del cuerpo humano por los accidentes del clima de Chile y de las costumbres chilenas? . . . Lo dicho se aplica a la mineralogía, a la geología, a la

teoría de los meteoros, a la teoría del calor, a la teoría del magnetismo; la base de todos estos estudios es la observación, la observación local, la observación de todos los días, la observación de los agentes naturales."

5. As Casey Blanton puts it, "American fiction and the American travel narratives that influenced it share a response to the idea of travel as a symbolic act, heavy with promises of new life, progress, and the thrill of escape" (18).

6. The Baudrillard/Žižek notion of "desert of the real" turns outward this classical and inward-looking concept of the desert, by concentrating on the manipulability of perception: after having existed for a long time in a convincing virtual simulacrum, the emancipated subject finds itself in the dismal "real" world—the true desert (Žižek 15). Within travel studies, sociologists like Dean MacCannell have critiqued the "staged authenticity" of the tourist experience (95–107).

7. These mendicants played a key role as forward agents of the feudalistic *encomienda* system of indentured servitude that would last for centuries. These men of the cloth seeded the landscape with ranchos, missions, and *reducciones,* where converted Indians—in their view, spiritual children needing guardianship—were taken under religious and economic tutelage and taught Western values, technologies, and trades in exchange for involuntary labor. This infantilization of a vast majority of the native population of the Americas initiated the persistent racial caste system that plagues Latin America to this day. The legal structure for this originated in the 1551 debates between Bishop Fray Bartolomé de las Casas, author of *A Short Account of the Destruction of the Indies* (1552), and the philosopher Juan Ginés de Sepúlveda. See Lewis Hanke's *All Mankind Is One* (1974) and the more recent *Darker Side of the Renaissance* by Walter Mignolo (1995); on the *encomienda* system, see *Encomenderos of New Spain* by Robert Himmerich y Valencia (1996).

8. Much of what remains of the nonphysical Aztec culture—its rituals, beliefs, habits, proverbs, and customs—is contained in the massive protoethnographic work of the Franciscan Bernardino de Sahagún (1499–1590), the *Historia natural* (known as the *Florentine Codex)*. Sahagún developed a system for collecting data that was astonishingly similar to modern ethnographic field methods. He interviewed, independently, two corroborating native sources before he accepted any information as definitive; he also employed Aztec scribes who were trained to understand and record information both in Aztec hieroglyphics and in Spanish. Other such examples stand out as well: the Dominican Francisco Ximénez (1666–1729), who learned Quiché language, was responsible for preserving the *Popol Vuj,* the Mayan sacred book.

9. In another such case from the colonial period, author William Byrd II gives two very different accounts of what can be found on the same trip: his very detailed narrative survey *History of the Dividing Line Betwixt Virginia and North Carolina* (1729) and his lewd *Secret History of the Dividing Line* (1841).

10. Clifford quips that Malinowski has "no method at all," alluding to Joseph Conrad's *Heart of Darkness,* which Clifford compares to Malinowski's

Diary: "Both *Heart of Darkness* and the *Diary* appear to portray the crisis of an identity—a struggle at the limits of Western civilization against the threat of moral dissolution" (98). In *Heart of Darkness,* when narrator Marlowe reads Kurtz's unsent report it becomes apparent to him that Kurtz has gone mad in the wilderness: into his otherwise balanced assessment of the natives, Kurtz has scrawled "exterminate all the brutes." Clifford astutely notes how both Malinowski the ethnographer and Kurtz the ivory trader/missionary endured lonely sojourns so unsettling that they reached a schizophrenic split.

11. A speculative field devoted to proving that Lewis's death was a murder has been quite productive; see John Guice, *By His Own Hand?*

12. This was studied by Angel Rama in his classic *The Lettered City* (77–78). It is hard to underestimate how many Latin American officials of all ranks—lawyers, presidents, ministers, and functionaries at all levels—have been published novelists or poets.

13. Bahktin elaborates: "Forming itself in an atmosphere of the already spoken, the word is at the same time determined by that which has not yet been said but which is needed and in fact anticipated by the answering word. Such is the situation with any living dialogue. The orientation towards an answer is open, blatant and concrete" (*Dialogic Imagination,* 279–80).

14. Cathy Davidson's *Revolution and the Word* and Irving Leonard's *Books of the Brave* make strikingly similar cases, looking at the books brought from home by the new arrivals, which shaped their image of what was before their eyes.

15. Oddly enough, the picaresque and the quixotic became inexorably intertwined, but literary criticism seems not to have made much of this genre trouble. When, and why, did the lonely rogue's tale become confused with the tale of the mythic and bickering *pair* of travelers? More important, why is this modal blurring significant? I will refer to some of these questions in the pages ahead.

16. Especially in the second part of *Don Quixote,* these parallel fantasy worlds are invented and staged by others, reflecting the Don's delusions as they were set out in part 1: Sancho is awarded the governorship of the "island" he had been dreaming about (and proves to be a surprisingly level-headed ruler) and the Don is challenged by "Knight of the White Moon," the disguised bachelor Sansón Carrasco (2:45, 2:64).

17. "*Homophilic* loyalties are enlisted as a source of security (for the state, the community, the citizen or ethical subject). Conversely, and much to the puzzlement of contemporary commentators, *philoxenic* solidarities introduce the disruptive category of risk into the otherwise determined Epicurean espousal of the ethical benefits of cultivated *ataraxia,* or invulnerability, and *autarkia,* or self-sufficiency. Any sort of friendship (local or global) is emotionally risky, as it might bedevil the tranquil Epicurean sage with anxieties of affective dependence. But friendships toward strangers or foreigners, in particular, carry exceptional risks, as their fulfillment may at any time 'constitute a felony *contra patriam*'" (Gandhi 29).

1. Fools of Empire

1. Instead of the standard English translation of the title (*El Lazarillo: A Guide for Inexperienced Travelers between Buenos Aires and Lima*, 1773), this is closer to the original *El lazarillo de ciegos caminantes desde Buenos-Ayres hasta Lima*, in which "ciegos caminantes" is literally "blind walkers" or "blind travelers." (The complete Spanish title is, comically, a paragraph long.)

2. The "true" picaresque is on several levels itself a nonconforming, "delinquent" literary genre. For instance, it is simultaneously critical and proud of the larger social forces it documents—nationalist criticism in Spain has always seen it as an instrument of empire, whereas the political left has claimed it as realistic critique of the institutions of discipline such as the church, and the privileged warrior class. Offering (mostly) a reversal to the standard Anglo-American appreciation of the optimistic late picaresque, Lennard Davis offers a compelling treatment of its connection with the "criminal" origins of the modern novel. Davis claims that during the seventeenth century, narrative began to announce itself as "purely factual or actually recent," and that this claim is tied to various "true" accounts of criminality, including journalistic ones (70): "There seems to have been something inherently novelistic about the criminal, or rather the form of the novel seems almost to demand a criminal content," and the novel, like the criminal, "is both locus of fraud and the locus of truth" (125, 128).

3. Anything coming from the other side of the Pyrenees was orientalized, a fetish that led to the German Romantics' sensualizing rediscovery of the Spanish Baroque, to exoticizing works like Prosper Merimée's (and later George Bizet's) *Carmen*, and to Washington Irving's *Tales of the Alhambra*. Spain was seen as a backward place of heat, bullfights, Catholic superstition, veiled women, honor killings, and delinquents. As argued above, the *Lazarillo* and *Don Quixote* do share a family resemblance. Both feature episodic structures and marginalized protagonists who wander through the underside of society; both offer a comic platform for social satire; and both avail themselves of unapologetic cruelty and "lower body humor," as Bakhtin called Cervantes's brand of Rabelaisian comedy (114). Neither the author of the *Lazarillo de Tormes* nor Cervantes inaugurated this sort of wandering episodic structure per se: it can be traced to classical sources such as Lucianic satire and Petronius's *Satyricon*, as well as to medieval saints' lives and confessions. Another shared element is purely practical: *Don Quixote*'s immediate models were popular chivalric adventure books meant to be read aloud to illiterate audiences, with chapters offering a good pause structure. See Matthew Garrett for a recent consideration of episodic structure in anglophone American literature.

4. This shared but radically contrasting relationship with truth claims has led some literary historians to place the two texts as ethical opposites: *Lazarillo* a protorealist text, a shining example of crudely effective mimetic chronicling, as Alexander Parker put it, "a boy who is a boy, not a miniature adult" (112), and on the other hand *Don Quijote* as the first modern and self-referential novel. Manuel Durán explores this at length in *La ironía en el Quijote*.

5. In North America, the relationship between the observation and description of nature and nation-building is long established. See *Early American Cartographies,* the useful volume edited by Martin Brückner on the cartography and spatialization of the entire American continent during this period.

6. On this topic, see Percy Adams's "Perception and the Eighteenth-Century Traveler."

7. See Vera Kutzinski and Ottmar Ettte on Humboldt and slavery ("Introduction," Humboldt 2001). The importance of Humboldt as a patron of the Americas runs deep within official national cultures: countless streets, parks, schools, counties, and even ocean currents are named after him and/or his fellow traveler, botanist Aimé Bonpland.

8. See Ilona Katzew's *Casta Painting*. Another example from the Spanish American seventeenth and eighteenth centuries where high art had a startling folk reinterpretation is the Baroque. The *barroco de indias* craftsmen produced numerous examples of architecture and decorative arts that were nativized and racialized. See Parkinson-Zamora (1997).

9. Cultural anthropologists like Arnold Van Gennep and Victor Turner who studied rites of passage define liminal space as a place outside of everyday norms where participants look back in. This upside-down, theatrical place is only temporary, since the liminal is built to be abandoned: initiates and revelers always return to society (Leach "Time").

10. Enrique Florescano and Isabel Sanchez further this view (183–290), as does John Lynch ("Origins" 13–30).

11. Claudio Veliz makes the intriguing case that turmoil resulting from the liberalization of trade initiated the dominant cultural and political trope of nineteenth-century Latin America, the dispute between *civilización* and *barbarie,* often simplified as a confrontation between an outward-looking, liberal, Europeanizing, urban (and urbane) ethos and a conservative, inward-looking, agrarian, and provincial one often allied with the church (125–162). This rift runs deep within the *gauchesque* literary genre discussed in the following chapter.

12. One possible counterreading regards the homegrown and the homemade, which began to replace goods from the mother country. This is perhaps where the backcountry found itself at the vanguard: it is the autochthonous place, its distance from the compromised metropolis necessitating self-sufficiency and, difficult as it was, forcing the imagining of independence. Two complementary studies, one about North America (Rigal's *American Manufactory*) and the other about Spanish America (Andrew K. Bush's *The Routes of Modernity*), explore the parallel between the commerce of manufactured, physical products and the commerce of culture. Bush argues that during the late colonial period in Spanish America, the native-spun and "coarse"—both words and cloth—began to flow from the periphery to the metropolis, gradually replacing the better-crafted European goods flowing in the other direction: the beginning of a postcolonial modernity (26–27).

2. Dying Pastoral

1. When I refer to the cultural construction, I use the term "cowboy"; when I refer to the historical figure I use terms such as "range driver." There is no analogue for the term "gaucho," although the "gauchesque" certainly refers to a cultural imaginary.

2. "The ruling class in the countryside had traditionally imposed a system of coercion upon people whom they regarded as *mozos vagos y mal entretenidos*—vagabonds without employer or occupation, idlers who sat in groups singing to a guitar, drinking maté, gambling, but apparently not working. This class was seen as a potential labor force and was therefore subject to all kinds of constraints and controls by the landed proprietors: punitive expeditions, imprisonment, conscription to the Indian frontier, corporal punishment, and other penalties" (Lynch, *Argentine* 104).

3. For generations, just about every leading Argentine intellectual, whether provincial or from the city, has found it necessary to argue for the *Martín Fierro* as the national foundational epic—for instance, Leopoldo Lugones (1874–1938) with *El payador* (*The gaucho singer*) or Ezequiel Martínez Estrada (1895–1964) author of, among other works, the massive *Muerte y transfiguración de Martín Fierro* (*Death and transfiguration of Martín Fierro*).

4. The widely available translation of *Martín Fierro* (1974) only contains "The Departure." An older (1936) out-of-print translation includes most of the "Return" (trans. Walter Owen). Much of this translation's print run is marred by mispagintion and printing errors. All excerpts from the "Return" use either the Owen translation where adequate (as indicated) or are my translation.

5. See Jens Andermann, "Argentine Literature."

6. Turner's triumphalist image was of a West where "every individual was a new Adam. Each was the first man, each the new unfallen," as Simonson writes (36). The frontier was the crucible where US national values of "frontierism. . . . free enterprise, laissez-faire, individual rights, natural rights, manifest destiny, popular nationalism, and social mobility" were born (37). The contrasting reading to this optimism argues that the "closing" marked a decline, according to more recent revisionists of Turnerism (see Richard Slotkin and Roderick Frazier Nash). Wherever American exceptionalism is concerned, the stakes are quite high.

7. As Ludmer, the most sophisticated analyst of the gauchesque, puts it: "That transparency (which is in part, a product of the theft of the past and of the convergence of multiple forces on one point) . . . can only be read from within the already constituted genre, from the perspective of the future and its convention" (4).

8. This recalls the Marxist philosopher Louis Althusser's notion of "interpellation," which locates the constitution of the subject at the precise moment when he or she is called by the authorities, the "police" ("Hey, you there!"). When the ideological state apparatus orders him or her to conform, to stand down—that is the precise instant the subject, responding to the call from overwhelming and instantaneous authority, becomes him- or herself: a political mirror stage. "[What]

I have called interpellation or hailing, and which can be imagined along the lines of the most commonplace everyday police (or other) hailing: 'Hey, you there!' Assuming that the theoretical scene I have imagined takes place in the street, the hailed individual will turn round. By this mere one-hundred-and-eighty-degree physical conversion, he becomes a subject. Why? Because he has recognized that the hail was 'really' addressed to him, and that 'it was really him who was hailed' (and not someone else)" (174).

3. The Size of Domesticity 1

1. Summarizing this aspect of 1950s culture, Griffin and Susman write: "Fullfilling those utopian dreams made the United States a success.... Ironically, however, this moment of triumph was accompanied by something disturbing: a new self-consciousness of tragedy and sense of disappointment" (19). A more light-hearted overview of Cold War paranoia, Michael Barson and Steven Heller's *Red Scared!*, deals with the fairly limited subset of anxious works that represented the object of anxiety directly: films such as *The Manchurian Candidate* (1962).

2. Several interrelated thought patterns emerged as a result of this conflation of scales. A sense of being watched pervaded: alien invasion fantasies, like the film *The Day The Earth Stood Still* (1951); tortured, voyeuristic works like Hitchcock's *Rear Window* (1951) and *Psycho* (1960); paranoid political psychodramas such as *The Manchurian Candidate* (1959); and the opened secrets of the *Kinsey Reports* (1948, 53). Spy and noir genres flourished under the shadow of Sputnik.

3. Another interesting parallel between Biedermeier and the 1950s in North America is that, later, once their myths of a peaceful, simpler life had been punctured by social unrest, both produced intense nostalgia.

4. In Nadel's analysis, the second half of the Cold War—the late 1960s and 1970s—connects to the rise of postmodernism: cultural and political dissatisfaction led to questioning the normativity and reliance on closed forms, and this laid bare some internal contradictions and hardened fictions (157–203).

5. After Francis Ford Coppola's production company, which owned the rights to *On The Road*, made several fruitless attempts to bring the book to film, it finally succeeded, with Salles directing.

6. There were many known instances during the Cold War in which the United States helped Latin American intellectuals on the left, offering them fellowships and academic positions and funding their magazines and other publication venues. At times the purpose was to undercut Soviet influence, while at other times it was to purchase information about political activities. And sometimes it was for outright bribery, to soften or silence hard-line anti-US positions. This has been studied at length, notably by Jean Franco in her fine *Decline and Fall of the Lettered City*, in which she offers a close reading of the complicated relationship between the Latin American intelligentsia, US information and cultural agencies, and the CIA.

7. Argentina would not benefit from the global postwar boom that occurred in most of the capitalist West, led by the United States. Perón's policy

of protectionism, meant to promote self-sufficiency in industrial and manufactured goods, had an unintended consequence during this period: agriculture was neglected, eroding what historically had been the cornerstone of the country's export economy. Thus began the "Argentine paradox" of economic decline in the second half of the twentieth century. The relevant statistics can be found at http://www.nationmaster.com/country-info/stats/Economy/GDP-per-capita-in-1950; see also Guido di Tella, *Political Economy of Argentina*.

8. Besides being considered a founder of Latin American "ethnomarxism," Mariátegui is often cited as one of the first ecologically aware social critics. The emphasis in his *Seven Essays* on the Indians' deep ties with the land, and their "correct" communitarian use of it, is seen as an expansion of dialectical materialism to include an awareness of the limits of natural resources—often overlooked in Marxism's utilitarian view of the material world as primarily a source of raw materials for the human endeavor (see Jorge Coronado's *Andes Imagined*, 25–52). During this same period, the postrevolutionary Mexican government was experimenting with small-plot land distribution to the recently emancipated peasant class, implementing a communal system, *ejidos*. This was something Mariátegui was likely observing, given his active exchanges with Mexican intellectual and political figures of the Mexican Revolution, such as José Vasconcelos (see Vásquez Castillo).

4. The Size of Domesticity 2

1. Kristine Vanden Berghe gives a fine overview of the main issues that arise when an educated, urban mestizo like Marcos assumes roles as spokesperson and leader in an indigenous rebellion (54–87). Jan de Vos, in *Una tierra para sembrar sueños* (2002), offers a good counterpoint, stating that the indigenous population had been reclaiming "the book" for quite a while before the appearance of the Zapatistas and Marcos. For a broader approach to the deployment of "Indianness" in the uprising at large and its various discourses (not just those of Marcos), a useful discussion is Nicholas Higgins's *Understanding the Chiapas Rebellion*; Thomas Olesen also lays out the discursive networks created by the movement.

2. Michael Tangeman writes that the *declaración* is "devoid of much of the leftist rhetorical baggage usually accompanying leftist Latin American guerilla movement" (89). Vanden Berghe, perhaps the most thorough formal reader of Marcos's narratives, notes that classical anti-US rhetoric is strangely muted in Marcos's voice, replaced by a wider-ranging, nuanced, and ironic stance (143–53).

3. Mariana Mora, who outlines the progression of Zapatista discourse from this early stage to the later "Otra Campaña," claims this "first moment" was where the indigenous-rights claims were predominant. Given its surprising success due to the novel use of media, it morphed into the terms of the larger struggle. "The decision to construct the autonomous municipalities generated" a "reinterpretation of the movement, originally conceived as primarily agrarian, as one that linked resource distribution to self-determination" (70). According to Mora, the two disparate aims—local resource distribution and indigenous

rights on the one hand, and self-determination in the face of a large system on the other—did not come into clearer synergy until the later stages of the movement in 2006, after almost "a decade of local practice." In any case, Marcos's ironic and playful language appeared as early as 1994. Josefina Saldaña-Portillo argues for a different reading of the development of Zapatista discourse: she addresses the complex signification of *mestizaje* within the discourse in tandem with parallel resistance movements, such as US Chicanismo. Saldaña-Portillo contends that the Zapatista shift away from a local agenda toward a larger one that engaged with national and even international concerns (e.g., political transparency and referendum initiatives, recall votes)—and, we can assume, antineoliberalism in general—was what caused the hard government backlash. The Zapatistas "exceeded the terms of their own subalternization," the "particularity of their ethnicity" (402–3).

4. Most of my references to the Spanish originals refer to the six-volume collected *Documentos y comunicados* (1994–2001), unless otherwise noted.

5. Spivak's position is somewhat polemical within the debate over essentialism, because she argues for the occasional *necessity* of essentialism by the resistance to power: "It's the idea of *strategy* that has been forgotten. . . . So long as the critique of essentialism is understood not as an exposure of error, our own or others', but as an acknowledgment of the dangerousness of *something one cannot not use*" (5, my emphasis).

6. Approaches to this range from short, mostly impressionistic journalistic pieces by notables Margo Glantz (1998), Gabriel Zaid (1994), and Hugo Hiriart (1995) to more theoretically inclined (e.g., Eduardo Duhalde and Enrique Dratman, 231–34). Most significant, perhaps, is Marcos himself.

7. As Griffin and Susman note, "Comics dramatized . . . the same kind of collective representation appearing in so many realms of postwar culture: heroic figure who is a concerned, anxious sinner capable of the most dreadful acts and incapable of operating rationally in terms of a scientific society's norms" (28).

8. According to Latin American literature specialist Hermann Herlinghaus, Marcos is not exactly an antihero, but rather an "anti-Platonic" half-hero who, through intentional inconsistency and discontinuity, seeks discursive emancipation from the mechanism of authorial voice, which is ultimately hegemonic. Like the unifying Foucauldian author function, the notion of the "hero" is suspect (225–28).

9. Border Arts performance artist Guillermo Gómez-Peña, for one, sees in the high-irony Subcomandante a fellow *performero* (90); "hacktivists" such as Electronic Disturbance Theater founder Ricardo Dominguez have claimed a seamless connection to Marcos's work (Fusco and Dominguez, 2010).

10. Herlinghaus couches Marcos's duality in Brechtian terms: "What we have is the 'Brechtian' problem regarding the relationship between those who 'make' history and those who 'write' it, those who move history and those who dedicate themselves to its symbolic ordering—between the 'who' and the 'what'"

(221, my translation). He argues that "Marcos has invented" his ironic persona "as a satirical postscript to a bourgeois project whose cultural hegemony" nonetheless "continues to echo" throughout it (57).

5. Doesn't He Ever Learn?

1. Here I follow ideas laid out by Edward Said in his meditation *On Late Style* (2006).

Works Cited

A Note on Translations: With the hope of including as many fellow travelers as possible who may lack a working knowledge of Spanish, as a practical concern I have tried to minimize the language barrier. It is fortunate that virtually all of the primary works exist and are readily available in good (or at least workable) English translations or subtitled films. For the most part I cite from these. In cases when they are inadequate or nonexistent, I give my own translation and note the exception. Thankfully, much of the history, theory, and criticism originally in Spanish is also available in English. Unfortunately, many of the primary texts in English do not yet exist in Spanish translation.

Adams, Percy. "Perception and the Eighteenth-Century Traveler." *Eighteenth Century* 26, no. 2 (1985): 139–57.
Adorno, Rolena. "The Negotiation of Fear in Cabeza De Vaca's Naufragios." *New World Encounters,* edited by Stephen Greenblatt, 48–84. Berkeley: University of California Press, 1993.
Althusser, Louis. *Lenin and Philosophy, and Other Essays.* London: New Left, 1971.
Anderson, Benedict. *Imagined Communities.* London: Verso, 1991.
Anderson, Jon Lee. *Che Guevara: A Revolutionary Life.* New York: Grove, 1997.
Anonymous. *The Life of Lazarillo De Tormes, His Fortunes and Adversities.* Translated by Harriet De Onís. Great Neck, NY: Barron's Educational Series, 1959.
Apter, Emily S. *Continental Drift: From National Characters to Virtual Subjects.* Chicago: University of Chicago Press, 1999.
Bakhtin, Mikhail. *Rabelais and His World.* Bloomington: Indiana University Press, 1984.
Barth, John. "A Literature of Exhaustion." *Atlantic Monthly,* August 1967, 29–34.
Bartolomé, Efraín. "War Diary." In *First World, Ha Ha Ha!: The Zapatista Challenge,* edited by Elaine Katzenberger, 5–28. San Francisco: City Lights, 1985.
Bello, Andrés. "Discurso Pronunciado Por El Rector De La Universidad De Chile En El Aniversario Solemne De 29 De Octubre De 1848." *Revista Anales* 7, no. 7 (2014): 276–306.

Berghe, Kristine, and Bart Maddens. "Ethnocentrism, Nationalism, and Post-Nationalism in the Tales of Subcomandante Marcos." *Mexican Studies/Estudios Mexicanos* 20, no. 1 (2004): 123–44.
Berlant, Lauren Gail. *Cruel Optimism.* Durham, NC: Duke University Press, 2011.
Bethell, Leslie. *Argentina since Independence.* New York: Cambridge University Press, 1993.
Blanton, Casey. *Travel Writing: The Self and the World.* Genres in Context. New York: Routledge, 2002.
Bolton, Herbert E. "The Epic of Greater America." *American Historical Review* 38 (1933): 448–74.
Borges, Jorge Luis, and Andrew Hurley. *Collected Fictions.* New York: Viking, 1998.
———. *Selected Poems.* New York: Viking, 1999.
Brackenridge, H. H. *Modern Chivalry.* Indianapolis: Hackett, 2009.
Brading, D. A. *The First Americans.* Cambridge: Cambridge University Press, 1991.
Brickhouse, Anna. *The Unsettlement of America: Translation, Interpretation, and the Story of Don Luis De Velasco, 1560–1945.* Imagining the Americas. New York: Oxford University Press, 2014.
Brückner, Martin, ed. *Early American Cartographies.* Chapel Hill: University of North Carolina Press, 2011.
Buñuel, Luis, dir. *Simon of the Desert.* 1965; Tujunga, CA: Foothill Video Home Entertainment, 2009. Video recording.
Bush, Andrew. *The Routes of Modernity: Spanish American Poetry from the Early Eighteenth to the Mid-Nineteenth Century.* Lewisburg, PA: Bucknell University Press, 2002.
Castiglia, Christopher. *Bound and Determined: Captivity, Culture-Crossing, and White Womanhood from Mary Rowlandson to Patty Hearst.* Women in Culture and Society. Chicago: University of Chicago Press, 1996.
———. *Interior States: Institutional Consciousness and the Inner Life of Democracy in the Antebellum United States.* New Americanists. Durham, NC: Duke University Press, 2008.
Cervantes, Miguel. *Don Quixote.* Translated by Walter Starkie. New York: Penguin, 1964.
Churchill, Winston. "The Sinews of Peace March 5, 1946." In *Winston S. Churchill: His Complete Speeches, 1897–1963,* edited by Robert Rhodes James, 7285–93. Vol. 7. New York: Chelsea House, 1974.
———. "We Shall Fight on the Beaches." June 4, 1940. https://winstonchurchill.org/resources/speeches/1940-the-finest-hour/we-shall-fight-on-the-beaches/.
Clifford, James. *Predicament of Culture.* Cambridge, MA: Harvard University Press, 1988.
Comaroff, Jean, and John Comaroff. "Millennial Capitalism: First Thoughts on a Second Coming." *Public Culture* 12, no. 2 (2000): 291–343.

Cornejo Polar, Antonio, and Roberto Paoli. "Sobre El Concepto De Heterogeneidad a Proposito Del Indigenismo Literario." *Revista de Crítica Literaria Latinoamericana* 6, no. 12 (1980): 257–67.

Coronado, Jorge. *The Andes Imagined: Indigenismo, Society, and Modernity.* Illuminations: Cultural Formations of the Americas. Pittsburgh, PA: University of Pittsburgh Press, 2009.

Cuarón, Alfonso, dir. *Y Tu Mamá También.* 2001; Beverly Hills, CA: Metro Goldwyn Mayer Home Entertainment, 2002. Video recording.

Cunha, Euclides da. *Rebellion in the Backlands.* Translated by Samuel Putnam. Chicago: University of Chicago Press, 1944.

Davidson, Cathy N. *Revolution and the Word: The Rise of the Novel in America.* Rev. ed. New York: Oxford University Press, 2004.

Davis, Lennard. *Factual Fictions: The Origins of the English Novel.* Philadelphia: University of Pennsylvania, 1996.

de Man, Paul. *Blindness and Insight; Essays in the Rhetoric of Contemporary Criticism.* Edited by Wlad Godzich. Minneapolis: University of Minnesota Press, 1983.

———. *The Rhetoric of Romaticism.* New York: Columbia University Press, 1984.

di Tella, Guido. *The Political Economy of Argentina, 1946–83.* Pittsburgh, PA: University of Pittsburgh Press, 1989.

Dorfman, Ariel, and Armand Mattelart. *How to Read Donald Duck: Imperialist Ideology in the Disney Comic.* New York: International General, 1975.

Duhalde, Eduardo Luis, and Enrique Dratman. *Chiapas, la nueva insurgencia: la rebelión Zapatista y la crisis del estado Mexicano.* Buenos Aires: Ediciones del Pensamiento Nacional, Distribución exclusiva Ediciones Colihue, 1994.

Durán, Manuel. *La ambiguedad en el Quijote.* Xalapa: Universidad Veracruzana, 1960.

Eagleton, Terry. *Walter Benjamin, or, Towards a Revolutionary Criticism.* London: Verso, 1981.

Ejército Zapatista de Liberación Nacional (Mexico), Carlos Monsiváis, and Elena Poniatowska. *EZLN: Documentos y comunicados.* Colección problemas de México. 5 vols. Mexico City: Ediciones Era, 1994–2001.

Emerson, Ralph Waldo. *Selected Writings of Ralph Waldo Emerson.* New York: Signet, 2011.

Fernández Armesto, Felipe. *The Americas: A Hemispheric History.* Modern Library Chronicles. New York: Modern Library, 2003.

Fiedler, Leslie. "Come Back to the Raft Ag'in, Huck Honey!" *Partisan Review* 15, no. 6 (1948): 664–71.

Fielding, Henry. *Tom Jones.* New York: Modern Library, 1985.

Fisher, John. "Imperial Free Trade and the Hispanic Economy, 1778–1796." *Journal of Latin American Studies* 13, no. 1 (1986): 21–56.

———. "The Imperial Response to 'Free Trade': Spanish Imports from Spanish America, 1778–1796." *Journal of Latin American Studies* 17, no. 1 (1985): 35–78.

Fitz, Earl. E. "Inter-American Literary Studies in the Early Twenty-First Century: The View from the United States." In *The International Turn in American Studies*, edited by Marietta Messmer and Armin Paul Frank, 103–28. Frankfurt am Main: Peter Lang, 2015.

Fliegelman, Jay. "American One-Sidedness: The Unrealizable Ideal of Democratic Conversation." In *The Concept and Practice of Conversation in the Long Eighteenth Century, 1688–1848*, 87–102. Newcastle: Cambridge Scholars, 2008.

Florescano, Enrique, and Isabel Gil Sánchez. "La época de las reformas borbónicas y el crecimiento económico, 1750–1808." In *Historia general de México*, edited by Daniel Cosío Villegas, 183–290. Vol. 2. Mexico: El Colegio de México, 1976.

Ford, John, dir. *The Searchers*. 1956; Burbank, CA: Warner Brothers Home Video, 1997. Video recording.

Foucault, Michel. *The Birth of the Clinic: An Archaeology of Medical Perception*. New York: Vintage, [1963] 1984.

———. "Of Other Spaces." *Diacritics* 16, no. 1 (1986): 22–27.

Franco, Jean. *The Decline and Fall of the Lettered City Latin America in the Cold War*. Convergences. Cambridge, MA: Harvard University Press, 2002.

Freleng, Isidore ["Friz"], dir. *By Word of Mouse*. 1954; Burbank, CA: Warner Brothers Pictures.

Frye, Northrop. *Anatomy of Criticism; Four Essays*. Princeton, NJ: Princeton University Press, 1971.

Fusco, Coco, and Ricardo Dominguez. "Ricardo Dominguez Interviewed by Coco Fusco." April 15, 2017. http://subsol.c3.hu/subsol_2/contributors2/domingueztext2.html.

Gandhi, Leela. *Affective Communities: Anticolonial Thought, Fin-De-Siècle Radicalism, and the Politics of Friendship*. Politics, History, and Culture. Durham, NC: Duke University Press, 2006.

García Márquez, Gabriel. *A Hundred Years of Solitude*. Translated by Gregory Rabassa. New York: Avon, 1971.

Garrett, Matthew. *Episodic Poetics: Politics and Literary Form after the Constitution*. New York: Oxford University Press, 2014.

Gennep, Arnold van. *The Rites of Passage*. Chicago: University of Chicago Press, 1961.

Gerbi, Antonello. *The Dispute of the New World*. Translated by Jeremy Moyle. Pittsburgh, PA: University of Pittsburgh Press, 1973.

Glantz, Margo. "Paz y Marcos: máscaras y silencios." *La Jornada Semanal*, September 20, 1998, https://jornada.com.mx/1998/09/20/sem-glantz.html.

Goethe, Johann Wolfgagng. *Scientific Studies*. Translated by Douglas Miller. New York: Suhrkamp, 1988.

Goldman, William. *William Goldman: Four Screenplays: With Essays,* Marathon Man, Butch Cassidy and the Sundance Kid, The Princess Bride, Misery. New York: Applause, 1995.
Gomez-Peña, Guillermo. "The Subcomandante of Performance." In *First World, Ha Ha Ha! The Zapatista Challenge,* edited by Elaine Katzenberger, 89–96. San Francisco: City Lights, 1995.
González Echevarría, Roberto. *Celestina's Brood: Continuities of the Baroque in Spanish and Latin American Literatures.* Durham, NC: Duke University Press, 1993.
———. *Myth and Archive: A Theory of Latin American Narrative.* Durham, NC: Duke University Press, 1998.
Griffin, Edward, and Warren Susman. "Did Success Spoil the United States? Dual Representations in Postwar America." In *Recasting America: Culture and Politics in the Age of Cold War,* edited by Lary May, 19–37. Chicago: University of Chicago Press, 1989.
Guevara, Che. *Guerilla Warfare.* Lincoln: University of Nebraska Press, 1998.
Guevara, Che, Brian Loveman, and Thomas M. Davies. *Guerrilla Warfare.* 3rd ed. Wilmington, DE: SR/Rowman & Littlefield, 1997.
Guevara, Ernesto, and Daniel James. *The Complete Bolivian Diaries of Ché Guevara: And Other Captured Documents.* New York: Stein & Day, 1968.
Guice, John D. W., ed. *By His Own Hand? The Mysterious Death of Meriwether Lewis.* Norman: University of Oklahoma Press, 2006.
Hanke, Lewis. *All Mankind Is One.* De Kalb: Northern Illinois University Press, 1974.
———. *Do the Americas Have a Common History? A Critique of the Bolton Theory.* Borzoi Books on Latin America. New York: Knopf, 1964.
Hardt, Michael, and Antonio Negri. *Empire.* Cambridge, MA: Harvard University Press, 2000.
Henck, Nick. *Subcommander Marcos: The Man and the Mask.* Durham, NC: Duke University Press, 2007.
Herlinghaus, Hermann. *Renarración y descentramiento: mapas alternativos de la imaginación en América Latina.* Madrid: Iberoamericana Vervuert, 2004.
———. "Subcomandante Marcos: Narrative Policy and Epistemological Project." *Journal of Latin American Cultural Studies* 14, no. 1 (2005): 53–74.
Hernández, José. *The Gaucho Martín Fierro.* Translated by Catherine Elena Ward. Albany: State University of New York Press, 1967.
———. *The Gaucho Martin Fierro.* Translated by Walter Owen. New York: Farrar & Rinehart, 1936.
Herzog, Werner, dir. *Fitzcarraldo.* 1982; Troy, MI: Anchor Bay Entertainment, 1999. Video recording.
Hill, Ruth. *Hierarchy, Commerce, and Fraud in Bourbon Spanish America: A Postal Inspector's Exposé.* Nashville: Vanderbilt University Press, 2005.

Himmerich y Valencia, Robert. *The Encomenderos of New Spain, 1521–1555.* Austin: University of Texas Press, 1991.

Hinderaker, Eric, and Peter C. Mancall. *At the Edge of Empire: The Backcountry in British North America.* Regional Perspectives on Early America. Baltimore, MD: Johns Hopkins University Press, 2003.

Hiriart, Hugo. "Máscaras Mexicanas." *Mitos mexicanos.* Edited by Enrique Florescano, 93–98. Mexico City: Aguilar, 1995.

Holden, Stephen. "Once Upon a Time in a Very Familiar West." *New York Times,* January 26, 2007.

Hubbard, Bill. *American Boundaries: The Nation, the States, the Rectangular Survey.* Chicago: University of Chicago Press, 2009.

Humboldt, Alexander von. *Personal Narrative of Travels to the Equinoctial Regions of America during the Years 1799–1804 by Alexander V. Humboldt and A. Bonpland.* Translated by Thomasina Ross. London: George Routledge & Sons, 1851.

———. *Vues des cordillères et monumens des peuples indigènes de l'amérique.* Large Folio. 20 Maps. Paris: F. Schoell, 1810.

Humboldt, Alexander Von, Vera M. Kutzinski, and Ottmar Ette, eds. *Political Essay on the Island of Cuba.* Chicago: University of Chicago Press, 2011.

Jamison, Kay Redfield. *Night Falls Fast: Understanding Suicide.* New York: Knopf, 1999.

Johnson, Denis. *Jesus' Son.* New York: Farrar, Straus & Giroux, 1992.

Kaiser, Walter. *Praisers of Folly.* Cambridge, MA: Harvard University Press, 1963.

Katzenberger, Elaine. *First World, Ha Ha Ha! The Zapatista Challenge.* San Francisco: City Lights, 1995.

Katzew, Ilona, et al. *Casta Painting: Images of Race in Eighteenth-Century Mexico.* New Haven, CT: Yale University Press, 2004.

———. *New World Orders: Casta Painting and Colonial Latin America.* New York: Americas Society, 1996.

Kennan, George. "Telegram, George Kennan to George Marshall [Long Telegram]." 1946. https://digitalarchive.wilsoncenter.org/document/116178.pdf.

Kermode, Frank. *The Sense of an Ending: Studies in the Theory of Fiction.* Mary Flexner Lectures. New York: Oxford University Press, 1967.

Kerouac, Jack. *On the Road.* New York: Penguin, 1976.

Krauze, Enrique. "Humboldt y México: un amor correspondido." *Vuelta,* July 1994, pp. 21–24.

Kristeva, Julia. *Revolution in Poetic Language.* New York: Columbia University Press, 1984.

Lackey, Kris. *Roadframes: The American Highway Narrative.* Lincoln: University of Nebraska Press, 1997.

Leach, E. R. *Rethinking Anthropology.* Monographs on Social Anthropology. London: Athlone, 1961.

Leland, John. *Why Kerouac Matters: The Lessons of on the Road (They're Not What You Think)*. New York: Viking, 2007.
Lewis, Meriwether, and William Clark. *The Journals of Lewis and Clark*. Boston: Houghton Mifflin, 1953.
Lezama Lima, José. *La expresión americana*. Edited by Irlemar Chiampi. Mexico City: Fondo de Cultura Económica, 1993.
Looby, Christopher. "The Constitution of Nature: Taxonomy as Politics in Jefferson, Peale, and Bartram." *Early American Literature EAL* 22, no. 3 (1987): 252–73.
———. *Voicing America: Language, Literary Form, and the Origins of the United States*. Chicago: University of Chicago Press, 1996.
Lowell, Robert. *Life Studies and for the Union Dead*. New York: Farrar, Straus & Giroux, 1967.
Ludmer, Josefina. *The Gaucho Genre: A Treatise on the Motherland*. Durham, NC: Duke University Press, 2002.
Lynch, John. *Argentine Dictator: Juan Manuel De Rosas, 1829–1852*. Oxford: Oxford University Press, 1981.
———. "The Origins of Latin American Independence." In *The Independence of Latin America,* edited by Leslie Bethell, 1–48. Cambridge: Cambridge University Press, 1987.
MacCannell, Dean. *The Tourist: A New Theory of the Leisure Class*. Berkeley: University of California Press, [1976] 1999.
Maclean, Alison, dir. *Jesus' Son*. 1999; Santa Monica, CA: Lions Gate Entertainment.
Malinowski, Bronislaw. *A Diary in the Strict Sense of the Term*. London: Routledge & Kegan Paul, 1967.
Marcos, and Acción Zapatista Editorial Collective. *Conversations with Durito: The Stories of the Zapatistas and Neoliberalism*. New York: Autonomedia, 2005.
———. *Relatos de el viejo Antonio*. Escritos Del Subcomandante Marcos. San Cristóbal de las Casas, Chiapas, México: Centro de Información y Análisis de Chiapas, 1998.
———. *The Story of Colors = La historia de los colores*. El Paso, TX: Cinco Puntos, 1999.
Mariátegui, José Carlos. *Siete ensayos de interpretación de la realidad Peruana*. Mexico City: Biblioteca Era, [1928] 1979.
Martí, José. *Our America: Writings on Latin America and the Struggle for Cuban Independence*. Translated by Elinor Randall. New York: Monthly Review, 1977.
May, Elaine Tyler. *Homeward Bound: American Families in the Cold War Era*. New York: Basic Books, 1988.
Mignolo, Walter. *The Darker Side of the Renaissance: Literacy, Territoriality, and Colonization*. Ann Arbor: University of Michigan Press, 1995.

Mora, Mariana. "Zapatista Anticapitalist Politics and the 'Other Campaign': Learning from the Struggle for Indigenous Rights and Autonomy." *Latin American Perspectives* 34, no. 2 (2007): 64–77.
Nadel, Alan. *Containment Culture: American Narrative, Postmodernism, and the Atomic Age*. New Americanists. Durham, NC: Duke University Press, 1995.
Nash, Roderick Frazier. *Wilderness and the American Mind*. Yale Nota Bene. 4th ed. New Haven, CT: Yale University Press, 2001.
Neruda, Pablo. *Canto General*. Translated by Jack Schmitt. Latin American Literature and Culture. Berkeley: University of California Press, 1991.
Nugent, Frank S. *The Searchers* (1956) shooting script. https://www.dailyscript.com/scripts/searchers.html.
Núñez Cabeza de Vaca, Alvar. *The Narrative of Cabeza De Vaca*. Lincoln: University of Nebraska Press, 2003.
Ochoa, John A. *The Uses of Failure in Mexican Literature and Identity*. Austin: University of Texas Press, 2004.
Ortega y Gassett, José. *Obras Completas*. Vol. 1. Madrid: Ed. Taurus/Fundación José Ortega y Gasset, 2004.
Parker, Alexander Augustine. *Literature and the Delinquent: The Picaresque Novel in Spain and 1599–1753*. Edinburgh: Edinburgh University Press, 1967.
Paz, Octavio. *The Labyrinth of Solitude*. Translated by Lysander Kemp. New York: Grove, 1961.
Pérez Firmat, Gustavo. *Do the Americas Have a Common Literature?* Durham, NC: Duke University Press, 1990.
Petzoldt, Paul K., and National Outdoor Leadership School. *The Wilderness Handbook*. New York: W. W. Norton, 1974.
Pratt, Mary Louise. "Humboldt y la reinvencion de America." *Nuevo texto critico* 1, no. 1 (1988): 35–53.
———. *Imperial Eyes: Travel Writing and Transculturation*. New York: Routledge, 1992.
Proulx, Annie. "Brokeback Mountain." *New Yorker,* October 13, 1997, 74–85.
Pynchon, Thomas. *Slow Learner: Early Stories*. Boston: Little, Brown, 1984.
Rama, Angel. *The Lettered City*. Translated by John Charles Chasteen. Post-Contemporary Interventions. Durham, NC: Duke University Press, 1996.
Rancière, Jacques. *Short Voyages to the Land of the People*. Atopia: Philosophy, Political Theory, Aesthetics. Stanford, CA: Stanford University Press, 1990.
Rigal, Laura. *The American Manufactory: Art, Labor, and the World of Things in the Early Republic*. Princeton, NJ: Princeton University Press, 1998.
Ronell, Avital. *Crack Wars: Literature Addiction Mania*. Texts and Contexts. Lincoln: University of Nebraska Press, 1992.
———. *Stupidity*. Urbana: University of Illinois Press, 2003.
Rotker, Susana. *Captive Women: Oblivion and Memory in Argentina*. Translated by Jennifer French. Cultural Studies of the Americas. Minneapolis: University of Minnesota Press, 2002.

Said, Edward W. *On Late Style: Music and Literature against the Grain.* New York: Pantheon, 2006.
Saldaña Portillo, Josefina. "On the Road with Che and Jack: Melancholia and the Legacy of Colonial Racial Geographies in the Americas." *New Formations* 47 (2002): 87–108.
———. "Who's the Indian in Aztlán? Re-Writing Mestizaje, Indianism, and Chicanismo from the Lacandón." *Nepantla: Views from South* 3, no. 2 (2002): 287–314.
Salles, Walter, dir. *The Motorcycle Diaries/Diarios De Motocicleta.* 2004; Universal City, CA: Focus Features Spotlight Series, 2005. Video recording.
———. "Notes for a Theory of the Road Movie." *New York Times,* November 11, 2007.
Sedgwick, Eve Kosofsky. *Between Men: English Literature and Male Homosocial Desire.* Gender and Culture. New York: Columbia University Press, 1985.
Sheehan, James J. *German History, 1770–1866.* Oxford History of Modern Europe. Oxford: Oxford University Press, 1989.
Shumway, Nicolas. *The Invention of Argentina.* Berkeley: University of California Press, 1991.
Simonson, Harold Peter. *The Closed Frontier: Studies in American Literary Tragedy.* New York: Holt, Rinehart, 1970.
Slotkin, Richard. *The Fatal Environment: The Myth of the Frontier in the Age of Industrialization, 1800–1890.* New York: Atheneum, 1985.
———. *Gunfighter Nation: The Myth of the Frontier in Twentieth-Century America.* New York: Maxwell Macmillan International, 1992.
———. *Regeneration through Violence: The Mythology of the American Frontier, 1600–1860.* Middletown, CT: Wesleyan University Press, 1973.
Spivak, Gayatri Chakravorty. *Outside in the Teaching Machine.* New York: Routledge, 1993.
Stafford, Barbara Maria. *Voyage into Substance: Art, Science and the Illustrated Travel Account, 1760–1840.* Cambridge, MA: MIT Press, 1984.
Stolley, Karen. *El Lazarillo de ciegos caminantes: un itinerario crítico.* Puertas 88. Hanover, NH: Ediciones del Norte, 1992.
Tangeman, Michael. *Mexico at the Crossroads: Politics, the Church, and the Poor.* Maryknoll, NY: Orbis, 1995.
Trotsky, Leon. *Literature and Revolution.* Translated by Rose Strunsky. New York: Russell & Russell, 1957.
Turner, Frederick Jackson *The Frontier in American History.* New York: Henry Holt, [1893] 1921.
Twain, Mark. *The Adventures of Huckleberry Finn.* New York: Bantam, 1981.
Vanden Berghe, Kristine. *Narrativa de la rebelión Zapatista: los relatos del Subcomandante Marcos.* Colección Nexos Y Diferencias no. 13. Madrid, Frankfurt am Main: Iberoamericana/Vervuert, 2005.

Vandera, Alonso Carrió de la [Concolorcorvo]. *El Lazarillo: A Guide for Inexperienced Travelers between Buenos Aires and Lima, 1773.* UNESCO Collection of Representative Works Latin-American Series. Bloomington: Indiana University Press, 1965.
Vasconcelos, José. *Memorias.* 2 vols. México City: Fondo de Cultura Económica, 1982.
Vázquez Castillo, María Teresa. *Land Privatization in Mexico: Urbanization, Formation of Regions, and Globalization in Ejidos.* New York: Routledge, 2004.
Veliz, Claudio. *The Centralist Tradition of Latin America.* Princeton, NJ: Princeton University Press, 1980.
Vos, Jan de. *Una tierra para sembrar sueños: historia reciente de la Selva Lacandona.* Sección de obras de historia. Mexico City: Centro de Investigaciones y Estudios Superiores en Antropología Social/Fondo de Cultura Económica, 2002.
Watts, Steven "Walt Disney: Art and Politics in the American Century." *Journal of American History* 82, no. 1 (1995): 84–110.
Weber, David J. *The Mexican Frontier, 1821–1846: The American Southwest under Mexico.* Histories of the American Frontier. Albuquerque: University of New Mexico Press, 1982.
White, Ed. "Introduction." In *Modern Chivalry,* edited by Ed White, ix–xxviii. Indianapolis: Hackett, 2009.
Williams, Raymond. *The Country and the City.* New York: Oxford University Press, 1973.
Zaid, Gabriel. "Chiapas: La guerrilla posmoderna." *Claves de la razón práctica* 44 (1994): 22–34.
Zamora, Lois Parkinson, and Monika Kaup. *Baroque New Worlds: Representation, Transculturation, Counterconquest.* Durham, NC: Duke University Press, 2010.
Zamora, Lois Parkinson. "Magical Ruins/Magical Realism: Alejo Carpentier, Francois De Nome, and the New World Baroque." In *Poetics of the Americas: Race, Founding, and Textuality.* Edited by Bainard Cowan and Jefferson Humphries, 63–103. Horizons in Theory and American Culture. Baton Rouge: Louisiana State University Press, 1997.
Žižek, Slavoj. *Welcome to the Desert of the Real! Five Essays on 11 September and Related Dates.* New York: Verso, 2002.

Index

Adventures of Augie March, The (Bellow), 38
Adventures of Huckleberry Finn, The (Twain), 38, 127
aesthetic form: and Cold War domesticity, 81–82; and historical change, 120–21; and "late" style, 142n1; New World Baroque, 11; scientific influence on, 42–43, 50–54
Alamán, Lucas, 44
Alfred P. Sloan Foundation, 107
Althusser, Louis: interpellation, 138n8
americanismo, 1, 42, 120
Anderson, Benedict: *Imagined Communities*, 35, 36, 53, 86
Apter, Emily, 20–21
Argentinian Constitution of 1853, 62
Argonauts of the Western Pacific (Malinowski), 19
Ascasubi, Hilario, 59
Auden, W. H., 79

backcountry: as comparative term, ix–x, 92–93; in cyberspace, 119; definition of, 6, 14; disappearance of, 6–10, 75; formation of, 9; knowledge of, 36, 43, 49; as literary setting, 32; and male friendship, 27, 87; Pampas, 62–65; relationship to European "mother" country, 11–13; relationship to metropolis, 2, 3, 9–11, 13, 24, 137n12; relationship to wilderness, 14, 17, 61–62, 75; as site of uprisings, 34, 96, 100; as transitional zone, 14, 17, 19, 62. *See also* metropolis; wilderness
Bakhtin, Mikhail, 136n3; carnival, 52; dialogism, 24, 25, 135n13

Barth, John, 121
Baudrillard, Jean: "desert of the real," 134n6
Bauer, Ralph, ix
Beat poets, 84–85. *See also* Kerouac, Jack
Bello, Andrés, 12–13, 42, 44
Berlant, Lauren, 130
Berry, Wendell, 8
Biedermeier (style): and Cold War–era domesticity, 81–82, 88, 139n3
biomes: ecotones, 14, 24; grasslands, 57
Blanton, Casey, 134n5
blindness: and insight, 125, 129–30; and scientific vision, 49; and stupidity, 49, 52; in travel literature, 33–36, 51
Bloom, Harold, 121
Bolaño, Roberto: *The Savage Detectives*, 87
Bolívar, Simón, 44
Bonaparte, Joseph, 54
Bonpland, Aimé, 43, 44, 137n7
Borges, Jorge Luis: "The Biography of Tadeo Isidoro Cruz," 69–70; "The Ethnographer," 28–29, 131; "Texas," 57, 64, 67, 76
Brackenridge, Hugh Henry: *Modern Chivalry*, 2, 3, 31–32, 50
Brading, David, 54
Brando, Marlon, 84
Bremer, Fredrika, 17
Brickhouse, Anna, ix, 8
"Brokeback Mountain" (Proulx), 72–74, 77, 131
Buffon, George-Louis Leclerc, comte de, 42, 43
Bundy, McGeorge, 103
Buñuel, Luis: *Simon of the Desert*, 14

Burnham, Frederick Russell: *Scouting on Two Continents*, 7
Burton, Richard: *The Arabian Nights*, 76
Buscón de Alfarache (de Queveda), 37
Butch Cassidy and the Sundance Kid (Hill), 78–79
Byrd, William, II, 134n9

Cabeza de Vaca, Álvar Núñez: *Narrative*, 14, 15–17, 23, 74–75
Cabrera, Miguel, 46–47, 50
Calderón de la Barca, Fanny, 17
Call of the Wild, The (London), 69
Campo, Estanislao del, 59
Candide (Voltaire), 32, 123
Cañizares-Esguerra, Jorge, ix; *Puritan Conquistadors*, x
Carrió de la Vandera, Alonso. *See* Vandera, Alonso Carrió de la
Castiglia, Christopher: *Bound and Determined*, 133n3
cartography. *See* mapping
casta (genre of painting): folk imitations of, 49–50, 51, 137n8; racial categorization, 45–50
Castro, Fidel, 119
Cervantes, Miguel de: *Don Quixote*, 3, 21–22, 31, 135n16, 136n3; "quixotic" literature, 25–27, 32–33, 37–39, 40
Charles III (Spain), 53, 56
Churchill, Winston: Cold War rhetoric, 82–83, 103–4, 114–15
civilización y barbarie, 1, 137n11. See also *Facundo: Civilization and Barbarism*
Clark, William, 20–21. *See also* Lewis, Meriwether
Clifford, James, 19–20, 50, 134n10
Cold War, 2; and American counterculture, 85; "containment" culture, 4–5, 27–28, 80–81, 85–86, 99; cultural anxieties and, 105–6, 109–10, 139nn1–2; and domesticity, 81–82, 83–84, 87; influence on Zapatista rhetoric, 114–15, 117, 119; masculinity in, 84; question of scale, 83, 87, 96, 102–3, 115; rhetoric of, 82–83, 99, 103–4, 105; and the "road" genre, 78–79, 87–88; role of technocrats in, 103–4; and superheroes, 112, 113–14
Comaroff, Jean and John, 116
Conrad, Joseph: *Heart of Darkness*, 134n10
Constitution of 1853 (Argentina), 62

Constitution of 1917 (Mexico), 96, 101, 118
"containment culture": in Cold War America, 2, 4, 27–28, 80–81, 113; domesticity, 83–84, 99; and "road" genre, 4–5, 85–86; and United States counterculture, 84–86. *See also* Cold War
Cooper, James Fenimore, 84
counterculture: in United States, 84–86; Zapatista movement as, 118–19
cowboys, 27; disappearance of, 3–4, 64–65, 67–69, 75; in literature, 59, 68–69; and male friendship, 27–28, 71–74; relationship to "gaucho" figure, 57–59, 137n1. *See also* gaucho; range driver
criollismo, 8, 68, 69. *See also* Spanish Decrees of Free Trade of 1778
criollos: and Spanish administrative reforms, 53–55
Cuarón, Alfonso: *Y Tu Mamá También*, 87
Cunha, Euclides da: *Rebellion in the Backlands*, 10–11

Darwin, Charles, 43
Davidson, Cathy, 35–36, 40, 55, 135n14
Davis, Lennard, 37, 136n2
Decline of the West, The (Spengler), 121
Decree of Free Trade of 1778. *See* Spanish Decrees of Free Trade of 1778
Defoe, Daniel: *Robinson Crusoe*, 22–23
de Man, Paul, 91, 129–30
dialogism, 135n13; in picaresque literature, 40–41; in solitary travel, 20, 101; in travel narratives, 24, 25
Disneyland, 82
Disney Studios, 107, 111–12
Dominguez, Ricardo, 141n9
Doña Bárbara (Gallegos), 8
Don Quixote, 21–22, 135n16; and knowledge, 26–27; and "quixotic" literature, 3, 25–26, 31–35, 36–39, 45–46, 51, 55, 120; versus the picaresque, 39, 135n15, 136n3
Don Segundo Sombra (Güiraldes), 8
Dorfman, Ariel: *How to Read Donald Duck*, 109
Durito (beetle): and cartoons, 108, 110; as fellow traveler, 5, 97, 99, 111; as professor, 101–2, 104–5, 115–16; and scale, 116–18

Eagleton, Terry, 52, 55
Easy Rider (Hopper), 79
Echevarría, Esteban, 133n3
ecotone, 14, 24
Ejército Zapatista de Liberación Nacional (EZLN), 98, 115, 117, 118
Elliott, Emory, 1
Emerson, Ralph Waldo, 12–13, 69
empire: during the Cold War, 2, 4; and colonial travel, 18, 25, 27, 55–56, 85; "empire without empire," 92, 119, 120; encroachment on the backcountry by, 60; end of, 121–22; and homosociality, 18, 75–76; and the metropolis, 12; and the picaresque, 35, 86, 136n2; and the "road" genre, 88, 92
Empire (Hardt and Negri), 62, 98
Ette, Ottmar, 43
EZLN (Ejército Zapatista de Liberación Nacional), 98, 115, 117, 118

Facundo: Civilization and Barbarism (Sarmiento), 9, 44, 59
Fernández Armesto, Felipe, 8
Fernández de Lizardi, José Joaquín: *The Itching Parrot*, 35
Fichte, Johann Gottlieb, 44
Fiedler, Leslie, 84
Fielding, Henry: *Joseph Andrews*, 37
Fisher, John, 55
Fliegelman, Jay, 41
Ford, John: *The Searchers*, 65, 70–72
Foreign Affairs, 84, 104
Foucault, Michel, 35
Fox, Emily, ix
Franco, Jean: *Decline and Fall of the Lettered City*, 139n6
Freleng, Isidore, 107, *108*
Frye, Northrop, 121
Fuentes, Carlos, 101
fuero, 53
Fuguet, Alberto: *Road Story*, 87

Gallegos, Rómulo; *Doña Bárbara*, 8
Gandhi, Leela, 27–28, 91, 124, 135n17
García Márquez, Gabriel, 10, 23; *One Hundred Years of Solitude*, 44, 65; *The Story of a Shipwrecked Sailor*, 14
gauchesque, x, 137n11, 137n1, 138n7; characters, 59; and the disappearance of gauchos, 68–69; and gaucho culture, 58–59; landscape, 68

Gaucho Martín Fierro, The. See *Martín Fierro*
gauchos, 27, 137n1; comparison with cowboys, 58, 74, 76, 91; disappearance of, 3–4, 8, 63–64, 67–69; and the *gauchesque*, 58–59; and male friendship, 27–28; in *Martín Fierro*, 60–62, 66, 69–70, 75; mythology of, 60, 67–68, 72. *See also* cowboys
Generall Historie of Virginia (Smith), 14
Gerbi, Antonello, 5; *The Dispute of the New World*, 41
Girard, René, 75
Goethe, Johann Wolfgang von, 45
Gómez-Peña, Guillermo, 141n9
Gonzalez Echevarría, Roberto, 23, 37
Gramsci, Antonio, 96
Granado, Alberto, 4, 88
grasslands, 3, 57, 63
Griaule, Marcel, 50–51
Griffin, Edward, 112, 139n1, 141n7
Guevara, Ernesto "Che": guerilla strategy, 94–95, 100, 102; *The Motorcycle Diaries*, 88; revolutionary rhetoric, 110–11, 116; as road tripper, 4, 88
Guice, John: *By His Own Hand?*, 135n11
Guide for Blind Travelers, A. See *El Lazarillo*
Guillén Vicente, Rafael Sebastián. *See* Marcos, Subcomandante
Güiraldes, Ricardo: *Don Segundo Sombra*, 8

Hanke, Lewis: *All Mankind Is One*, 134n7
Hardt, Michael, 62, 98, 116
Henck, Nick, 115
Heredia, José María, 42
Herlinghaus, Herman, 100–101, 141n8, 141n10
Hernández, José: *Martín Fierro*, 58–62, 65–66, 69, 71, 74–75
Hidalgo, Bartolomé, 59
Hill, George Roy: *Butch Cassidy and the Sundance Kid*, 78–79
Hill, Ruth, 36, 54
Himmerich Y Valencia, Robert: *Encomenderos of New Spain*, 134n7
Hinderaker, Eric: *At the Edge of Empire*, 6
homosexuality: in "Brokeback Mountain," 72–74, 76–77; in Cold War–era United States, 84; in homosocial relationships, 75

Index

homosociality: as effect of travel, 27–28; and empire, 18; as triangle, 17–18, 75–76, 87
Hopper, Dennis, 79
Howl (Ginsberg), 79
How to Read Donald Duck (Dorfman), 109
Hubbard, Bill, 13, 36
Huckleberry Finn. See *Adventures of Huckleberry Finn*
Humboldt, Alexander von, 25, 42, 137n7; and American nationalism, 44; *Political Essays*, 43; scientific observation, 44–45, 51; *Views of Nature*, 43; *Vues des Cordillères*, 43

Ibarra, José de, 47–49
Imagined Communities (Anderson), 35, 53, 86
Inordinate Eye, The (Zamora), 11
Interstate Highway System (United States), 82
Into the Wild (Krakauer), 14
Itching Parrot (Lizardi), 35

Jamison, Kay Redfield, 20
Jefferson, Thomas, 21, 42; *Notes on the State of Virginia*, 41
Jesus' Son (Johnson), 38; "ordinariness," 130–31; as picaresque narrative, 122–27; post-trauma, 128–29
Jesus' Son (Maclean), 122, 125, *130*
Johnson, Denis: *Jesus' Son*, 122–31
Johnson, Samuel: *Rasselas*, 32
Joseph Andrews (Fielding), 37

Kaiser, Walter, 26
Kennan, George: Cold War mentality, 84, 104, 105, 111, 114–15
Kennedy, John F., 103
Kermode, Frank, 23–24
Kerouac, Jack: *On the Road*, 4, 79, 85–86, 87, 88
Kondori, José, 11
Krakauer, Jon: *Into the Wild*, 14
Krauze, Enrique, 44
Kristeva, Julia, 74

Labyrinth of Solitude, The (Paz), 112
Lackey, Kris, 86
Las Casas, Bartolomé de, 134n7

"late" style, 121–22
Lazarillo, El: A Guide for Blind Travelers (Vandera), 3, 39–40, 60; and "empire," 53–56; as quixotic literature, 31–33, 39–40; stupidity in, 50, 51–52; as travelogue, 33–34, 36
Lazarillo de Tormes. See *Life of Lazarillo de Tormes*
Leonard, Irving: *Books of the Brave*, 135n14
Lewis, Meriwether, 20–21, 135n11
Lewis and Clark. See Clark, William; Lewis, Meriwether
Lezama Lima, José, 11
Life of Lazarillo de Tormes, 21; and *Jesus' Son*, 123; and *On the Road*, 86; relationship to "quixotic" genre, 25–26, 37–38, 136nn3–4
Lisboa, Antônio Francisco, 11
Little House series (Wilder), 7
Lolita (Nabokov), 79
Looby, Christopher, 41
London, Jack: *Call of the Wild, The*, 69
Looney Tunes, 107–8. See also Warner Bros.
Lowell, Robert, 79–80
Ludmer, Josefina, 68–69, 76, 138n7
Lukács, György, 121
Lussich, Antonio, 59

MacCannell, Dean, 135n6
Maclean, Alison: *Jesus' Son*, 122, 125, *130*
Malinowski, Bronislaw, 19–20, 21, 134n10
Mancall, Peter: *At the Edge of Empire*, 6
manifest destiny, 1, 138n6. See also Turner, Frederick Jackson
Mariátegui, José Carlos (*Seven Interpretative Essays*), 93–94, 140n8
Martí, José, 10, 42, 110
Martín Fierro (Hernández), 4, 138n4; Borges rewriting of, 69–70; cultural assimilation in, 66; domestication of gauchos, 65–66; and gauchesque genre, 58–59; interpretations of, 138n3; pair formation in, 61, 71–72; as reaction to modernization, 60, 62–63; wilderness in, 74, 75
mapping, 13, 136n5; Rectangular Survey System, 36; and scientific description, 42–43

Marcos, Subcomandante: cartoons and, 108–10, 111–12; Cold War rhetoric and, 99, 102–3, 104–6, 114–16; rhetoric of, 96–97, 98, 100–102, 110–11, 116–19; *The Story of Colors*, 109; as superhero, 112, 114–15; as traveler, 5; true identity of, 99. *See also* Durito
May, Elaine Tyler, 80–81
Meditations on Quixote (Ortega y Gassett), 26
Melville, Herman, 84
mendicant religious orders, 18, 134n7
metropolis: and American relationship to Europe, 12–13; knowledge-gathering and, 15, 19; relationship to backcountry, 2, 9–11, 24, 62–63, 67–69, 76, 137n12; as site of empire, 54–55, 60, 119; travel to and from, 5, 19, 22, 28–29
Mexican Constitution of 1917, 96, 101, 118
Mexican Revolution of 1910, 98, 115, 116, 140n8
Mignolo, Walter: *Darker Side of the Renaissance*, 134n7
Modern Chivalry (Brackenridge), 2, 3, 31; and dialogism, 40–41; as picaresque literature, 35–36; as quixotic literature, 3, 31–33, 37; setting, 31; stupidity, 37, 50, 51–52; as travelogue, 33–34, 51
Mora, Mariana, 140n3
Moreiras, Juan, 59
Motorcycle Diaries, The (Salles): intertextuality in, 92–93; Latin American context of, 89; political awakening, 91–92; and "road" genre, 87–88

Nabokov, Vladimir: *Lolita*, 78
Nadel, Alan, 4, 80, 99, 139n4
NAFTA, 55, 97–98
Napoleon I, 54
Narrative of Cabeza de Vaca, The, 14, 15–17, 23, 74–75
Nash, Roderick Frazier, 5
National Outdoor Leadership School, 31
Naturphilosophie, 42, 44
Negri, Antonio, 62, 98, 116
neoliberalism: NAFTA, 55; and Zapatista rebellion, 101, 102, 104–5, 115–16, 118, 140n3
Neruda, Pablo, 78, 86; *Canto General*, 93
Newman, Paul, 78

Nietzsche, Friedrich, 131
Nine Inch Nails, 120
Notes on the State of Virginia (Jefferson), 41
novelas de la tierra, 8

One Hundred Years of Solitude (Márquez), 44, 65
On the Road (Kerouac), 4, 79; connection to the picaresque, 86; domestic containment in, 85, 87, 89–91; homosocial triangulation in, 90–91; relationship to *Motorcycle Diaries*, 88, 91–93
On the Road (Salles), 87, 139n5
Ortega y Gassett, José, 26

Pagden, Anthony, 54
Pampas: as backcountry, 62–65; parallel with the US West, 3–4, 57–59, 64–65, 133n3. *See also* backcountry; the West (United States)
Parkinson-Zamora, Lois, ix, 11
Parks, Rosa, 84
Pauw, Cornelius de, 42
Paz, Octavio, 112
Peale, Charles Willson, 41
Perón, Juan, 89, 139n7
picaresque, 2; definition of, 136n2; dialogism in, 40; and empire, 35–36; *Jesus' Son* as, 122, 125, 131; and *On the Road*, 86; relationship to "quixotic" genre, 25–26, 33, 37, 38–39, 45–46, 120, 135n15; as story of escape, 22; as testimony, 37–38, 45–46, 125, 129
picaro: in *Jesus' Son*, 122–23, 125–26, 127, 128–29, 131; at margins of society, 35–36; as solitary traveler, 25, 39, 51, 124
Pinal, Silvia, 14
Polar, Antonio Cornejo, 25, 43, 44, 50–51
Political Essays (Humboldt), 43–44
Pratt, Mary Louise, 25, 43–44
Presley, Elvis, 84
Proulx, Annie: "Brokeback Mountain," 72–74, 77
Puritan Conquistadors (Cañizares-Esguerra), x
Pynchon, Thomas, 79, 81, 85–86

Quevedo, Francisco de: *Buscón de Alfarache*, 37

158 Index

Quiroga, Juan Facundo, 59
quixotic literature (genre): dialogism in, 40–41; relationship to picaresque, 25–26, 37–39, 120, 135nn15–16, 136n3; and scientific vision, 35–37, 41–43, 51–52, 55–56; and travel literature, 31–35; and truth claims, 38–39, 136n4

Rama, Angel: *The Lettered City,* 135n12
Rancière, Jacques, 120
range driver, 137n1; comparison to gauchos, 57–58, 67–69; disappearance of, 3–4, 67–69; and male friendship, 72–74, 76–77. *See also* cowboys; gauchos
Rasselas (Johnson), 32, 123
Raynal, Guillaume, 42, 43
Rectangular Survey System, 36
Redford, Robert, 78
Reed, Lou, 127, 129
relación (genre), 15
Reyes, Alfonso, x
Rivera, José Eustasio; *The Vortex,* 8
road genre, 27–28; in Cold War America, 4–5, 78–79, 84; homosociality in, 87; in Latin America, 79, 87–88; *The Motorcycle Diaries,* 93; *On the Road,* 4, 79; quixotic literature and, 3; Subcomandante Marcos and, 5, 115
Road Story (Fuguet), 87
Robertson, William, 42
Robinson Crusoe (Defoe), 22–23, 131
Ronell, Avital, 26–27, 51, 127
Rotker, Susana: *Captive Women,* 133n3
Rugendas, Johann Moritz: *El rapto,* 64

Sahagún, Bernardino de: preservation of Aztec culture, 134n8
Said, Edward: *On Late Style,* 142n1
Saldaña Portillo, Josefina, 92, 140n3
Salles, Walter: *The Motorcycle Diaries,* 87–88, 93; *On the Road,* 87, 139n5
Sandinistas, 98, 110
Sarmiento, Domingo Faustino: American exceptionalism, 42; *Facundo: Civilization and Barbarism,* 9, 44, 59
Savage Detectives, The (Bolaño), 87
Schelling, Friedrich Wilhelm Joseph von, 44
Schlesinger, Arthur, 103
Scouting on Two Continents (Burnham), 7

Searchers, The (Ford): backcountry domestication in, 65, 67; pair formation in, 70–72
Sedgwick, Eve Kosofsky, 17–18, 24, 75–76, 87
Sense of an Ending, The (Kermode), 23–24
Sepúlveda, Juan Ginés de, 134n7
Seraphim Falls (Ancken), 68
Seven Interpretative Essays (Mariátegui), 93–94
Sheehan, James, 81
Shining Path, 98, 101, 110
Simon of the Desert (Buñuel), 14
Slotkin, Richard, 8
Smith, John: *Generall Historie of Virginia,* 14
Spain: exoticization of, 136n3
Spanish Decrees of Free Trade of 1778, x, 53–55
Speedy Gonzalez, 106
Spengler, Oswald, 121
Spivak, Gayatri, 111, 141n5
Stafford, Barbara, 42–43, 45
Sterne, Laurence: *Tristram Shandy,* 32
Story of a Shipwrecked Sailor, The (García Márquez), 14
stupidity: as epistemological category, 26–27, 127; of picaros, 123; quixotic literature and, 25–26, 33–35, 36–37; and scientific vision, 49–52; traveling pairs and, 27, 124
Susman, Warren, 112

Tangeman, Michael, 140n2
"Taming of the Wilderness" (*conquista del desierto*), 63–65
Thelma and Louise, 17
Thoreau, Henry David: *Walden,* 14–15
Tristram Shandy (Sterne), 32, 34
Tropic of Cancer (Miller), 79
Trotsky, Leon, 22
Truman, Harry, 103
Truman Doctrine, 104
Turner, Frederick Jackson, 6–7, 8, 67, 138n6
Turok, Antonio, 97
Twain, Mark, 10, 84; *The Adventures of Huckleberry Finn,* 38, 127

Vanden Berghe, Kristine, 100–101, 115, 140nn1–2

Vandera, Alonso Carrió de la: career as inspector, 54, 55–56; as character, 39–40; *El Lazarillo*, 3, 31–36, 39–40, 50–52, 55–56
Vasconcelos, José, 133n3
Veliz, Claudio, 137n11
Velvet Underground, 127
Views of Nature (Humboldt), 43
Voltaire (François-Marie Arouet): *Candide*, 32
Vortex, The (Rivera), 8
Voto, Bernard de, 20, 21
Vues des Cordillères (Humboldt), 43

Walden (Thoreau), 14–15
Warner Bros., 106, 107, 109, 111
Watts, Steven, 107
Wayne, John, 70
West, the (United States): closing of the frontier, 67–68, 138n6; and gaucho culture, x, 67–69; mapping of, 36; parallels with the Pampas, 3–4, 57–58, 62–65; range drivers, 67–69; "road" genre and, 86–87; shifting location of, 7, 9. *See also* backcountry; cowboys; Pampas; range driver
Whiskey Rebellion, 11, 12
White, Ed, 40
Wilder, Laura Ingalls; *Little House* novels, 7

wilderness: and gaucho culture, x, 61–62; male bonding, 70–71, 74–76; and metropolis, 5; as site of self-discovery, 14–17, 21, 27, 28–29, 135n10; taming of, 63–65, 69; versus backcountry, 6–8, 9, 14, 62. *See also* backcountry; metropolis
Williams, Raymond: *The Country and the City*, 133n2
Wilson, Woodrow, 103

Ximénez, Francisco: preservation of *Popol Vuj*, 134n8

Y Tu Mamá También (Cuarón), 87

Zamora, Lois Parkinson: *The Inordinate Eye*, 11
Zapata, Emiliano, 98, 116
Zapatista uprising (1994–96), 96–102, 105–6, 108, 110; Marxism in, 101; relationship to previous movements, 98, 116–17; rhetoric of, 96–97, 98, 100–102, 104–5, 108–12, 115–19; stakes of, 97–98, 118, 140n3; Subcomandante Marcos, 99–102, 105–6, 118–19; use of masks in, 112, 114–15. *See also* Marcos, Subcomandante
Žižek, Slavoj: "desert of the real," 134n6

Recent books in the series
New World Studies

The Quebec Connection: A Poetics of Solidarity in Global Francophone Literatures
Julie-Françoise Tolliver

Comrade Sister: Caribbean Feminist Revisions of the Grenada Revolution
Laurie R. Lambert

Cultural Entanglements: Langston Hughes and the Rise of African and Caribbean Literature
Shane Graham

Water Graves: The Art of the Unritual in the Greater Caribbean
Valérie Loichot

The Sacred Act of Reading: Spirituality, Performance, and Power in Afro-Diasporic Literature
Anne Margaret Castro

Caribbean Jewish Crossings: Literary History and Creative Practice
Sarah Phillips Casteel and Heidi Kaufman, editors

Mapping Hispaniola: Third Space in Dominican and Haitian Literature
Megan Jeanette Myers

Mourning El Dorado: Literature and Extractivism in the Contemporary American Tropics
Charlotte Rogers

Edwidge Danticat: The Haitian Diasporic Imaginary
Nadège T. Clitandre

Idle Talk, Deadly Talk: The Uses of Gossip in Caribbean Literature
Ana Rodríguez Navas

Crossing the Line: Early Creole Novels and Anglophone Caribbean Culture in the Age of Emancipation
Candace Ward

Staging Creolization: Women's Theater and Performance from the French Caribbean
Emily Sahakian

American Imperialism's Undead: The Occupation of Haiti and the Rise of Caribbean Anticolonialism
Raphael Dalleo

www.ingramcontent.com/pod-product-compliance
Lightning Source LLC
Chambersburg PA
CBHW021357300426
44114CB00012B/1262